T0331418

Kerry Carson, PhD
Paula Phillips Carson, PhD

Defective Bosses
Working for the
"Dysfunctional Dozen"

Pre-publication
REVIEWS,
COMMENTARIES,
EVALUATIONS . . .

"**A** fantastic read! Much like the infamous 'Dirty Dozen,' the so-called 'dysfunctional dozen' represent a proverbial murderers' row of the types of bosses one can expect to encounter in any work setting. They represent every employee's worst nightmare, and unfortunately, are not all that rare. *Defective Bosses* provides not only a description of the various types and how to spot them, but helpful strategies on how to deal with each type. For those new to the work scene or for seasoned employees, the information provided in *Defective Bosses* could help save your career (or at least your sanity)."

David D. Day, PhD
Associate Professor
of Industrial/Organizational
Psychology,
Penn State University

More pre-publication
REVIEWS, COMMENTARIES, EVALUATIONS . . .

"**A**n excellent book for those in the early stages of their careers."

Alfred A. Bolton, DBA
Archivist, Management History,
Academy of Management,
Danville, VA

"**C**arson and Carson have written a clear and concise analysis of one of the major issues affecting employees today—dysfunctional bosses. . . . An insightful book for both practitioners and business people."

Gary D. Bruton, PhD
Assistant Professor,
Texas Christian University

"**I** have been employed since the age of thirteen. My formal entrance into the full-time workforce began with I turned twenty-one. Although most of my work experience has been in health care, I have been exposed to many bosses in my different jobs, from being a shoe shine boy in a pool hall to working as a first assistant to a neurosurgeon.

I have been a boss, but mostly an employee. This book has a refreshing insight into the types of bosses one may encounter; I have had bosses from every category. Even if your immediate supervisor is a good boss, the trickle-down effect from his or her 'defective boss' could make for an uneasy work environment.

This work is timely and timeless. With today's rapidly changing business structures, one is apt to face new bosses more often, whether one changes jobs or the job changes bosses. After reading this book, I was better able to diagnose, or categorize, the various bosses that I have had, and currently have.

Both authors are well-known to me. I am on my third round of formal education, spanning four decades. I have had many and varied professors. I have experienced both authors in my current round of education. Both are extremely dedicated and committed to their profession—the Science of Management. This book is an excellent vehicle, allowing others to be exposed to their academic insights and wisdom."

Phil L. Guillory, RN, BSN, CEN
President, Louisiana Council
of Emergency Nurses Association,
Eunice, LA

The Haworth Press, Inc.

Defective Bosses
Working for the
"Dysfunctional Dozen"

HAWORTH Marketing Resources
Innovations in Practice & Professional Services
William J. Winston, Senior Editor

New, Recent, and Forthcoming Titles:

Defective Bosses
Working for the
"Dysfunctional Dozen"

Kerry Carson, PhD
Paula Phillips Carson, PhD

The Haworth Press
New York • London

The Haworth Press, Inc., 10 Alice Street, Binghamton, NY 13904-1580

Cover design by Marylouise E. Doyle.

Library of Congress Cataloging-in-Publication Data

Carson, Kerry D. (Kerry David), 1946-
    Defective bosses : working for the "dysfunctional dozen" / Kerry Carson, Paula Phillips Carson.
        p. cm.
    Includes bibliographical references and index.
    ISBN 0-7890-0580-8 (alk. paper).
    1. Supervisors. 2. Managing your boss. 3. Personnel management. 4. Interpersonal relations. 5. Supervision of employees. I. Carson, Paula Phillips, 1967-   . II. Title.
HF5549.12.C375   1998
658.3'02—dc21   0-7890-0581-6   98-18463
                                                                                        CIP

To our son, David, for enriching our lives

ABOUT THE AUTHORS

Kerry David Carson, PhD, is Professor of management at the University of Southwestern Louisiana in Lafayette, specializing in organizational behavior. Prior to receiving his PhD, he worked as a therapist in a variety of psychiatric settings. His last position before entering academia was as a clinical director for a mental health center. His research interests include dysfunctional behavior in the workplace and career management.

Paula Phillips Carson, PhD, teaches human resources management and labor relations at the University of Southwestern Louisiana in Lafayette. She has received several awards for excellence in instruction and research, and she has published five books and over 100 articles. She is an active officer in the Academy of Management and provides seminars on management/employee relations.

CONTENTS

Preface

For Those Who Fear That Nothing as Rational as a Book Can Help Them Deal with Their Irrational Boss

"Berserk," "demented," "deranged," "insane," "off-balanced" —these are just a few of the characteristics that the employees we interviewed used to describe their bosses. Many other terms were equally descriptive, but were . . . well, let's just say, not fit to print. If you are ever running short of juicy cocktail conversation, no need to resort to rehashing the well-debated topics of religion or politics—just ask people about their bosses. We predict that you'll discover others are not only willing, but anxious, to unleash their repressed frustrations and accumulated hostilities. At least that was our experience.

After suffering through our share of subpar bosses, we began to wonder if our unfortunate experiences were unique. So we asked. Without much (if any) prompting, we heard horror stories of bosses who timed workers' bathroom visits, who regularly threw pencil sharpeners at employees' temples, or who ran away when they saw staff members approaching their offices. This is the stuff books are made of, we thought.

So we began to scour the library and the bookstores, looking for sage advice on how to deal with the "legion of lunatics" who had somehow clawed or wormed their way up the organizational ladder. To make a long story short, we found advice—but it hardly qualified as sage. Common recommendations included "quit your job" or "go right over your boss's head."

Such recommendations are easily written and perhaps even tempting. But in the real world, they are difficult to do, limited by such practical concerns as how will we eat dinner next Thursday, how will I pay my child's tuition in the spring, or how will I find another job now that I am known as a "troublemaker?" What is needed, we believed, is a surefire, fail-safe roadmap for detouring around defective bosses so that in the end, the victim is not the one penalized. That is what we intend to accomplish in this book—a how-to, how-not-to, why, and why-not guide for the journey into the inner workings of the defective boss's world.

PROFILING THE DYSFUNCTIONAL DOZEN

The "dysfunctional dozen" were selected for inclusion because we feel these personalities represent the most common profiles of defective bosses. We reached this conclusion based on many personal interviews, observations, and interactions with "crazy" leaders. In addition, we extensively researched the psychology and psychiatric literature for insights into these personality flaws. But unlike most medical sources, we did not focus on why or how the defects were developed (the only exception being where the causes of the flaws were laughable or otherwise just plain unbelievable!). We didn't much concern ourselves with overly protective mothers, abusive father figures, or childhood abandonment. Although these incidents may truly be tragic, we decided on a different starting point. Our focus was: My boss has the defect. How do I deal with it here and now?

The book is organized into three major parts, with four chapters in each. The first part identifies "Self-Centered Bosses"—those who are out for numero uno and who don't really care where you are so long as you are below and behind them. Self-centered bosses include the narcissists, sociopaths, paranoiacs, and histrionics. The second part describes "Controlling Bosses"—those who thrive on dominating you and will do it through any means possible. Controlling bosses include the authoritarians, obsessive-compulsives, explosives, and passive-aggressives. The third part focuses on "Neurotic Bosses"—those who seem far too pathetic to be leaders and who, frankly, may not even be together enough to follow. Neurotic bosses include the masochists, dependents, depressives, and anxious-avoidants.

Each profile included in *Defective Bosses* is discussed in a single chapter. Each chapter is divided into four sections: Deciphering the

Defect, Predictable Reactions to the Pathology, When the Defective Boss Looks in the Mirror, and Prescriptions for Persevering.

Deciphering the Defect

In this initial section, we introduce readers to the basic characteristics of the defect. How does this defective boss behave? How does he or she communicate? How does he or she react? This section will help the reader to identify which defect (or defects) contaminates the boss. At the end of this section, there is a self-test for the employee to take. It is called "Diagnosing the Defect," and consists of ten questions. If you can answer "yes" to at least seven of these questions, you can be quite sure that the defect has infiltrated your boss. The questions in the quizzes are based on observable behaviors, that is, you don't have to crawl inside the boss's mixed-up head or have long personal dialogues to answer these questions. They are simple, straightforward, telltale signs.

Predictable Reactions to the Pathology

If the first section in the chapter describes your boss, the second section is likely to describe you. Here we identify the most common, natural, and inborn responses employees experience in reaction to the defective boss's antics. But more important, we discuss how these innate reactions to the boss's disabling defect are likely to submerge you deeper into the quagmire of ineffective behaviors. Many times, employees unknowingly behave in a self-defeating manner that reinforces the leader's flaws. In this section, we show how and why this happens.

When the Defective Boss Looks in the Mirror

Military generals have long known that the best way to conquer enemies is to learn how they think, what makes them tick, and how they perceive the world. The same strategy can be used with defective bosses. When they are alone, inside their dark, bizarre private world, what is going on inside them? To have this knowledge goes a long way toward knowing how to deflect the defect. Many times, the defective boss's actions and personal thoughts are not in sync. If you respond to them solely on the basis of their observable behaviors, you may be way off the mark. Instead, when you understand what gets them going and what puts them at ease, half the battle is won.

Prescriptions for Persevering

In this final section, we offer constructive, practical, and doable tips for diffusing and dealing with a defective boss. It should be noted at this point that this book is written for one purpose only, that is, to save the sanity of those working under defective bosses. It is not our mission to help you "cure" your defective boss. Nor is it our intention to help the defective boss "cure" himself or herself. In some cases, that would require intense one-on-one therapy, with the boss positioned on the psychiatrist's couch rather than in the leather chair of the executive suite. In other cases, to expect a cure would be a futile dream. Instead, our sole aim is to help employees maneuver through the minefields laid by the defective boss. So, in this section, we offer tips on how to work around and even through the lunatic leader—with the ultimate objective of protecting yourself.

Interspersed through each chapter are graphic, sometimes amusing, sometimes disturbing anecdotes offered by many who suffer at the hands of defective bosses. Although the names have been changed to protect the guilty and the victimized, the bizarre scenarios haven't. Numerous contributors to the book gave permission for their stories to be used, but chose to remain anonymous. The following individuals, after disguising their supervisors' names, indicated their willingness to be acknowledged for case adaptations. These contributors, our students between 1995 and 1997, are: Michael Barrera, Dawn Brown, William W. Burgin III, Barbara Cage, Sergio Casanova, Laveta Collins, Daniel Crespell, Marc Crespell, Debra Dollins, Linda G. Ellis, Laura Flores, Scott Hanright, Harold Honegger, Susan Morris, Erika Munter, Thomas Nichols II, Ricardo Ortiz, Rebecca Patrick, Patricia Pena, Carlos Perez, Wally Perez, Harvey Salinas, Lalena Sanchez, Rudolph G. Soliz, Stephen C. Tagilabue, Tim B. Teas, Jeremy S. Tilton, and Mindy Wright.

We hope as you read through these vignettes, you won't recognize yourself—but we bet you will! Now for more discouraging news. If you think you have identified your boss in Chapter 4, don't stop there. Read on to Chapter 5. Most defective bosses are inflicted with more than one personality flaw. So, it is more than likely that you will recognize your boss again later in the book. But fear not, each chapter offers its own unique survival tips.

Introduction

*In each human heart are a tiger, a pig, an ass, and a nightingale.
Diversity of character is due to their unequal activity.*

Ambrose Bierce

WHY WE WIND UP WITH DEFECTIVE BOSSES

Each and every day we have exactly 86,400 seconds at our disposal. On average, 30,600 seconds are spent at work; 5,400 are spent traveling to and from work; 3,600 are spent preparing for work; and 7,200 are spent thinking (or worrying) about work. This adds up to a grand total of more than half our day—not including time spent finishing projects at home, attending "mandatory" social events, or complaining about our bosses. Now think about it—we don't spend our "nonworking" half of the day with crazy people. So why do we have to spend our "working" half with them?

Virtually all of us have, at one time or another, worked for someone else. And chances are, most of us have worked for at least one defective boss. A lucky few have only been exposed to one or two. But others seem to hopscotch from one defective boss to another. You may begin to wonder, "Is there something wrong with me that I can't find a sane place to work?"

Chances are, it is not you. Unless, of course, you have allowed one or more of your mad managers to push you over the edge. Unfortunately, sanity, experience, and ability do not always have much to do with promotion to a management position. Other irrelevant factors are often given much more credence. Bosses are sometimes picked because they are second cousins of the CEO; or they were in the same fraternity as one of the vice presidents; or they didn't demand a big salary increase with their promotion; or they were lucky enough to be

1

in the right place at the right time; or they were so poor at doing their jobs that the higher-ups had to do something with them. None of these reasons are rational. All of them are very real.

This discouraging state of affairs is problematic because work is an important part of who we are. When we are introduced to others, it often goes something like, "This is Kelly, an engineer at Polymar Tech." We become one with our jobs. Our personal and social identity is wrapped up in them. But this doesn't necessarily mean that we like what we do, or where we do it, or who we do it for.

Through our research, we haven't found many people who are totally satisfied with every aspect of their work situation. People complain about job security. They complain about their dirt-poor pay. They complain that their opinions are not respected. But most of all, they complain about their bosses. Defective supervision has encouraged unionization, sabotage and embezzlement, low productivity, and even violence.

The problem is, most of us work for people that we would never pick out or (privately) call our friends. We would never voluntarily go to dinner with them, make trips with them, or call them to chat. Unfortunately, we don't pick our bosses—we inherit them with the job. Unlike our husbands or wives, bowling teammates, or golf partners, we interact with our bosses because we have to—not because we choose to or want to. Experts estimate that two-thirds of all people selected for all positions are wrong for the job. And no laws, or scientific research, or popular books seem to be helping to improve this deplorable situation. So we are left with the undesirable realization that we just have to bite our lips, hold our tongues, grit our teeth, and persevere.

My father taught me to work; he did not teach me to love it.

Abraham Lincoln

Although most bosses are "normal" most of the time, many seem to be "off the mark" with enough frequency to make us suspect that they suffer from some underlying pathology. And our suspicions are likely correct. Business has no lock on sanity. In fact, the pressurized environment created by "downsizing," "restructuring," "rightsizing," "reengineering," or whatever the current buzz-word is creates an atmosphere perfect for the defective boss's idio-syncrasies to creep out.

Unfortunately, you and your peers are likely to have the best van-tage point for observing your defective boss's grotesque and outlandish actions. This is because pathology is most likely to be unleashed on those who are in less powerful positions, on those who are not really postured to do anything about it. And while your boss's personality flaws may seem painfully destructive to you, you will likely have a hard time convincing others about your intolerable plight.

In fact, some personality defects seem to be conducive to getting ahead in the world of work. Higher-ups may see your boss's aggres-sive tendencies as healthy competitiveness—you likely see it as brutal-ity. Higher-ups may see your boss's meticulous tendencies as thor-oughness—you likely see it as picayune. Higher-ups may see your boss's confidence as intelligence—you likely see it as egocentric. So any complaints, criticism, or objections may be interpreted as sour grapes or jealousy.

But in reality, we know there is a difference between effective and defective people—those who are effective are at the normal end of the continuum while those who are defective are at the pathological end. Herein lies an important point. Pathology is a matter of degree. Very, very few (if any at all) individuals are the perfect picture of mental health. So even those classified as "effective" people are sometimes angry or sullen or suspicious. But . . . they are not consistently that way.

Effective people have the flexibility to adapt their style to fit the situation. Defective bosses do not. After working for them for a while, you will realize that they use the same dysfunctional style over and over again. They are myopic and distort the world to fit their fictional perception of reality. It is as if they wear tainted glasses that delude them from seeing things as they really are. Sometimes their singular worldview may be appropriate to the situation. Most of the time, it is not.

In the following table, we summarize the defective bosses who are most skilled at making the workplace agonizing. These are the profiles that will be dealt with in the remainder of the book.

PERSONALITY TYPES AND ASSOCIATED SYMPTOMS

Self-Centered Bosses

Narcissistic Boss	grandiose and entitled
Sociopathic Boss	unethical and manipulative
Paranoid Boss	suspicious and cold
Histrionic Boss	dramatic and seductive

Controlling Bosses

Authoritarian Boss	domineering and dogmatic
Obsessive-Compulsive Boss	stiff and perfectionistic
Explosive Boss	aggressive and volatile
Passive-Aggressive Boss	stubborn and antagonistic

Neurotic Bosses

Masochistic Boss	tormented and self-doubting
Dependent Boss	submissive and obliging
Depressive Boss	distressed and pessimistic
Anxious Boss	fearful and avoidant

SECTION ONE:
SELF-CENTERED BOSSES

He that won't be counseled can't be helped.

Benjamin Franklin

–1–

The Narcissistic Boss:
The "What-I-Want-Most-Is-to-Be-Worshipped" Type

Other people are quite dreadful. The only possible society is oneself.

Oscar Wilde

DECIPHERING THE DEFECT

Narcissistic bosses are, quite simply, egomaniacs. They are self-absorbed to the point of arrogance. They exhibit an insatiable desire for attention and admiration, and they have a compelling need for others to recognize their superiority. The narcissist is the type that must always be right—whether he or she is pontificating about the introduction of a new product, reduction of the federal deficit, or the athletic superiority of a favorite basketball team.

While these self-centered traits may wear thin on those who work for a narcissist, these same traits can facilitate the climb up the organizational ladder. Narcissists speak with an air of confidence and self-assurance. They remain calm in the face of crises, and they do not hesitate to take credit for workplace successes—whether or not they deserve the credit. It is, therefore, common to see narcissists occupying positions of authority in the workplace.

> Mark is the newly appointed Assistant Area Engineer at our local office of the State Highway Department. He has only been here for two weeks, yet even before he came, Mark's reputation preceded him. He was touted as a brilliant engineer,

a high-volume producer, and a real workaholic. In short, he was considered by those upstairs to be quite a talent. Since he has been here, we have all discovered he is talented. He's talented at snowing the execs, at buffaloing them—he has them brainwashed. They think Mark can walk on water, and he thinks he can, too. We just keep wondering how anyone can believe all the self-aggrandizing propaganda Mark spreads about himself. *(junior engineer, female, age 26)*

Narcissists are grandiose. They have an overinflated sense of their own self-importance and self-worth, and they leap to the conclusion that others should sublimate their personal needs and goals to attend to them. Because they feel innately superior, narcissists expect special consideration and treatment from everyone they come into contact with—from subordinates, to clients, to their auto mechanics and dry cleaners. Narcissists feel, in one word, entitled.

He was the type who would get up from his desk, walk out to the secretary's office, and ask her to file a folder in the cabinet that is right behind his chair. He could have filed it in two seconds—in a lot less time than it took him to ask the secretary to do it. But he liked to come out of his office and loudly issue commands. I think it made him feel important. He was starved for attention, for recognition. And his hunger was never satisfied. *(insurance salesperson, female, age 32)*

Narcissists demand to be the center of attention in every situation and they are opinionated to the point of being deaf to others' suggestions. They operate under the unwavering conviction that they, and they alone, are right. "I" and "me" are always preferred to "we" or "us." Narcissists long to be admired, praised, respected, and envied. To make sure this happens, they will grasp for more power, more status, and more money. They cherish the financial resources necessary to acquire symbols of success—such as sprawling homes, expensive imported cars, and fancy doodads such as portable computer/fax/photocopier combos. In fact, narcissists are somewhat of a paradox—although they have a very inflated ego, they also need accolades from others. This may make narcissists appear dependent, but they are not. While they will accept praise, narcissists have little regard for other's opinions. Narcissists can't really depend on anyone because of their underlying doubt of others' talents and their need to look down on others.

> Ramiriz, the Chief of Police, was difficult on the best of days. He felt he was "God" and didn't hesitate to remind the rest of us that we weren't. Chief Ramiriz's feelings of superiority manifested in many ways. But most especially, he was fond of belittling you in front of others. He would say things such as, "Are you suffering from a rectopticalidis?"—which meant he thought your optical nerves and rectum were crossed. *(dispatcher, male, age 34)*

Narcissists expect to be loved for the unique qualities they believe they possess. They convince themselves that they are, in reality, special. Fantasies of grandiosity preoccupy their thoughts. Their accomplishments are unrealistically overrated, yet at the same time, the narcissist's ambitions are never satisfied. Although appearing energetic, they are competitive, exhibitionistic, smug, and selfish. They may at first appear dignified, but most soon learn this is attributable to the narcissist's underlying vanity and feelings of superiority.

> Josh is the manager of the men's department in the store where I work. His favorite personal stories revolve around some type of self-admiration. His conversations seldom deviate from that subject. Josh tends to surround himself with others who can appreciate his incredible attributes as well as he can—if that is possible. *(retail clerk, female, age 19)*

Diagnosing the Defect: Is Your Boss Narcissistic?

YES	NO		
_____	_____	1.	Does your boss have an overinflated sense of his or her self-importance?
_____	_____	2.	Is your boss preoccupied with illusions of unlimited success, power, or intelligence?
_____	_____	3.	Does your boss demonstrate a lack of concern and awareness about others' problems?

YES   NO

_____   _____   4.   Does your boss act entitled to special treatment and favors?

_____   _____   5.   Is your boss constantly fishing for compliments about his or her greatness?

_____   _____   6.   Does your boss seem contemptuous of negative evaluations of his or her work by others?

_____   _____   7.   Does your boss believe that his or her problems are so unique that they can only be understood by special others?

_____   _____   8.   Is your boss overly grandiose about his or her accomplishments?

_____   _____   9.   Does your boss take credit for your accomplishments?

_____   _____   10. Is your boss an exhibitionist?

If you answered "YES" to more than 7 questions, your boss exhibits strong narcissistic tendencies.

If you answered "YES" to between 4 and 7 questions, your boss exhibits moderate narcissistic tendencies.

PREDICTABLE REACTIONS TO THE PATHOLOGY

When taken in small doses, narcissists can be quite entertaining, even charming. It is a common initial reaction to be overwhelmingly impressed by their eminence. The casual observer can easily equate their air of self-assurance with competence and charisma. To those who decide about promotions, the narcissist may be perceived as possessing extraordinary powers of persuasion and creative genius. Employees with low self-esteem are also likely to be taken in by the narcissist. In fact, some become disciples—defending to their death the narcissist's leadership abilities. These workers respond to the narcissist with unquestioned respect and obedience.

But most, even those who initially admired the narcissist, eventually realize the egomaniac is exaggerating his or her self-importance. Sooner or later, the narcissist will appear immodest and pretentious. Irritation then takes over. One's gut reaction is to try to burst the narcissist's balloon—to expose him or her—to let out all that hot air.

> Pat is an officer in the United States Navy. When Pat walks into the room, it's like roaches when the light gets turned on. Her overbearing presence makes it difficult for employees to even approach her with suggestions for improving productivity. Instead, we have learned that Pat is more interested in boasting about her athletic abilities—which she exaggerates far beyond reality. First of all, Pat is every bit of 5'2" tall and weighs 145 pounds. These are not necessarily the statistics that make up a world-class volleyball player. But to hear her, you would think she retired from pro ball and took up the military as a hobby. *(aviation trainer, male, age 27)*

As time wears on, though, irritation is likely to turn into anger. Employees come to realize that their relationships with the narcissist lack depth. The narcissistic boss can't empathize or recognize how others feel about a situation. He or she can't take joy in others' pleasures, and can't feel sympathy for others' pains.

Even worse, narcissists are extremely exploitative. While the narcissist fully expects special favors from employees, he or she feels no need to reciprocate. Therefore, it is common to feel taken advantage of. The narcissist does take others for granted. He or she lacks personal integrity and is not above fabricating—or telling outright lies—to preserve an image.

> Marissa, my supervisor, is like a two-year-old walking around in a woman's body. She eats up a lot of our valuable work time expounding about her fictional exploits, so I can't get my work done. And if that isn't bad enough, when I finally do have time at work to come up with something novel, she steals my idea. It's like these ideas come to her through divine inspiration or something. *(greeting card designer, female, age 37)*

The narcissist is also likely to be a rule breaker, the type that believes policies were formulated for everyone but him or her. So the narcissist is not likely to be concerned about attendance or tardiness. In fact, the narcissistic boss may not be around much. He or she often becomes involved with external professional associations, community activities, consulting, or some other high-profile activity where his or her exposure will be increased.

The narcissistic boss doesn't like details. Details are trivial issues that waste the narcissistic boss's magnanimous talent. Instead, particulars are delegated so the boss can concern himself or herself with more "important" issues. But rest assured, this boss not only delegates details, he or she also delegates responsibility for failures. Narcissists accept accolades for successes but distance themselves from misfortunes.

Narcissistic bosses cannot tolerate negative feedback—from anyone. They consider criticism to be a direct attack on their self-image. And, they react to criticism with rage and humiliation. Their estimation of the evaluator plummets. But narcissists are most likely to mask these violent reactions behind a facade of cool indifference. They implode rather than explode. But . . . the narcissist doesn't forget.

Working for a narcissist is likely to stifle your creativity and initiative. After all, why bother trying?

> The worst boss I ever worked for was Roger. He was above average in intelligence. Unfortunately, someone must have informed him of that at an early age. Regardless of the topic, he had an opinion. Since he would always belittle us, we stopped making suggestions. In fact, to be honest, we got sloppy about our work. But that only reinforced Roger's perception that he was far superior to us. It was a lose-lose situation. Within weeks, literally, a top-performer would devolve into an incompetent fool. Roger was like an infection. Once he contaminated the organization, the disease was extremely persistent. It just festered and continued to take hold, even after Roger was promoted to another facility. The healing process will take a long time, I'm afraid—even though the virus has finally been removed. *(software developer, male, age 39)*

One of two things invariably happens when the boss is narcissistic. Either: (1) the narcissist will criticize your work as being sloppy and sophomoric, or (2) the narcissist will take credit for your accomplishments. Instead of feeling guilty about basking in others' limelight, the narcissist simply concludes, "Wow! I really inspired her" or "Gee! I taught him well."

> Randi's favorite two "sports" were trapshooting and foxholing. Trapshooting refers to the idea that, "the only good ideas are the ones I have." Foxholing, also known as CYA, is a pattern of digging and ducking during turbulent times. Times were definitely turbulent. Randi was also quite skilled at purse-snatching. She had an uncanny ability to show up just at the right time and steal my ideas. *(systems engineer, male, age 31)*

Predictably, narcissists are horrendous in teams. Sharing the spotlight does not come easily to the narcissist. But the narcissist doesn't mind if fans congregate in his or her shadow. Like a sheepdog rounding up the flock, the narcissistic boss can easily sense those who are perceived to be appropriately responding. Employees who are submissive and servile will likely be taken into the narcissist's inner circle—or fan-club. Because these employees are rewarded by the narcissist, many will be tempted to "please the boss's' at any cost—even though doing so may not be in the best interest of the employing organization. When this happens, priorities get screwed up, inter-office competition becomes the norm, and once competent workers are transformed into brainless robotic "yes-people." All the while, this stroking fertilizes the narcissist's ego.

WHEN THE NARCISSISTIC BOSS
LOOKS IN THE MIRROR

Looking in the mirror is an activity that the narcissist will savor. The problem is that what the narcissist sees is someone truly believed to be superior to all others. The narcissist is not putting on an act. All that boasting, all that bravado, all that bull reflects how narcissists see themselves.

> I was teaching my class—about twenty minutes into my lecture, and in walks Joe, all puffed up and oblivious to the fact that he was interrupting. Without even a glance in my direction, Joe started handing back papers to the students that had just left his class and come to mine. When I started to protest, Joe quipped, "Well, what you're talking about can't be as important as me giving out my grades." How can you even argue with a person like that? *(professor, female, age 56)*

As obnoxious as narcissists are, they have been around since the beginning of time. In fact, the term "narcissism" evolved from classical Greek mythology. Narcissus spurned the love of his suitor, Echo. Because of this, the gods punished him by making him fall in love with himself. One day, Narcissus was wandering past a pond when he caught a glimpse of his reflection. He was so enamored by his image that Narcissus couldn't tear himself away. He was forever doomed to gaze at himself. There, at the edge of the pond, Narcissus died. Then he was changed into the flower that bears his name and grows at the edge of springs.

In reality, everyone is a little narcissistic. Don't we all linger over our reflection a little longer than required to comb our hair or shave? Don't we all enjoy tooting our own horn sometimes? There is nothing wrong with this. In fact, it is healthy. Some psychotherapy treatments actually attempt to instill narcissistic traits in patients with low self-esteem or masochistic tendencies. Even the popular press encourages narcissism. Books such as *The Art of Being Selfish* and *Looking Out for Number One* increase the legitimacy of self-absorption. But there is a line between health and pathology—and narcissists have crossed way over that line.

Mental health experts disagree on the causes of narcissism. Some theories attribute narcissism to parental rejection. In this scenario, the narcissist learns early on to trust only himself or herself and to love himself or herself above all others.

> Larry sees himself as superior. I can testify to that because I happen to work out at the same health club where he does. I notice him put on the additional weights whenever other engineers are in the vicinity. His actions—trying to always impress

others—make we wonder if he has any self-worth at all. *(engineer, male, age 28)*

Other theories attribute narcissism to parental overvaluation. Thus, narcissists are socialized to expect special treatment. But whatever the cause, the effects can be intolerable.

Narcissists have blind faith in the perception that their personal worth far exceeds anybody else's. And this exaggerated sense-of-self bolsters their feelings of optimism. A narcissist's mood is often untroubled, relaxed, and lighthearted. They suffer from few internal conflicts. Narcissists are so convinced they are special that this assumption is never questioned. Narcissistic bosses treat themselves kindly—self-gratification is a normal part of the narcissist's existence. They revel in their perceived charm, intelligence, and ability.

Although narcissists can brush off skeptics as being ignorant, they experience optimal gratification when employees worship them. But narcissistic bosses don't expect to have to do much to earn such adoration. In fact, narcissistic bosses believe that employees should feel honored and grateful just to work under the supervision of such an incredible leader.

PRESCRIPTIONS FOR PERSEVERING

To the healthy employee, narcissistic bosses appear condescending, narrow-minded, contemptuous, and pig-headed. But you can't change them. And they don't want to change themselves. They are pleased with their exalted station. The best you can do is skillfully maneuver around them in pursuit of peaceful co-existence. The following guideposts are offered to assist you in your trip.

Close the Door but Open a Window

The narcissist is very capable of making bad decisions—big, bad decisions. The challenge is to not let the narcissist lead you blindly down a failing course of action. This means that sometimes you will have to assert yourself to avoid going down with a sinking ship that is steered by a captain who is oblivious to the encroaching danger.

> One of Lew's favorite sayings was, "If that was a good idea, I would have thought of it myself." And that's the way it was. If he considered the situation a problem, he would have already addressed it. Therefore, there were never any problems—according to Lew. *(architect, male, age 48)*

Whether or not you will be able to save the ship will depend upon your approach—your tactics. Combative or chiding tactics will not work. Challenges to the narcissist's superiority can provoke vindictiveness and contempt. When employees are aggressive, narcissistic bosses are quick to take the offensive. They immediately devalue others' ideas and intellect. The harder an employee pushes, the more the narcissist becomes convinced that he or she is right and the naysayers are wrong. In addition, the narcissist is masterful at developing rationalizations and alibis to regain perfection in his or her eyes.

The trick is to not condemn, but to subtly offer alternative suggestions. Better yet, plant the seed in the narcissist's brain and let him/her sprout viable alternatives. That way, the narcissist can save the day—and think it was he or she insight that made it possible. Statements such as, "I see there are cost overruns on the Beta Project. I wonder if simplifying the design might decrease expenses," are likely to work better than, "I knew your design changes would make costs skyrocket. We are going to have to change them back." Condemnation threatens the narcissist. Alternatives give the narcissist a face-saving way out.

Settle into the Supporting Actor/Actress Role

It is important to the narcissistic boss that he or she never gives up center stage. Costars are not even tolerated. The best you can hope for is to share in the narcissist's applause. If you contribute to making that applause possible, the narcissist will develop a soft spot in his or her heart for you. The idea is to buy some time, develop your skills, learn what you can from the narcissistic boss, and settle for shared credit for your ideas until there is a good opportunity to move on.

> Come to think of it, I did take something valuable away with me after my experience with Linda. I learned about physics from her.

She taught me that elephantine egos can quickly expand to fill the space available. *(social worker, male, age 33)*

Become a Closet "Yes-Person"

No one likes a brown-nosed bootlicker—except a narcissistic boss. The narcissist is a "me-person" who rewards "yes-people." So swallow your pride (and disgust) and laugh at their jokes, compliment their superb taste in fashion, and dawdle over their brilliant insights. Remember, the narcissist can be kind and generous to those who inflate his or her ego.

But monitor yourself to make sure that your display of overly dramatic exaltation is private rather than public. If not, you will quickly become the brunt of office jokes. Even co-workers who are engaging in the same ingratiating tactics will become disdainful, and when you need the support of your peers, they will be nowhere in sight.

Give Credit When Credit Is Due

Narcissists have many bad points, but they may also have a couple of good ones. Narcissists will likely be hard-working, high-volume producers. Outperforming others earns them additional bragging rights. Narcissists are also likely to pay keen attention to the superiority of their output. In fact, they will simultaneously seek to avoid criticism of their own work while pointing out the errors and flaws in others' work. When efforts are directed toward the accomplishment of organizational goals, narcissists, like anybody else, should be recognized.

Don't Let Narcissism Become Contagious

Narcissism is not usually contagious. But it can infect you. It is often difficult to avoid a war of words with the narcissist. After growing weary of the narcissists' one-upmanship, you will likely be tempted to play some one-up yourself. But it is a game you cannot win. The opponent is too practiced, too skilled. In this regard, there is one good thing to be said about working for a narcissist—it forces you to not be one.

2

The Sociopathic Boss:
The "I'm-So-Slick, You-Don't-Even-Know-I'm-Doing-You-In" Type

The Devil can cite Scripture for his purpose.

William Shakespeare

DECIPHERING THE DEFECT

Since childhood, we have been warned to be wary of the "wolf in sheep's clothing." But there are so many wolves—so many sociopaths—and they are very skilled at hiding their true nature behind a well-crafted guise. This is why most sociopaths work and live among us, instead of being incarcerated behind steel bars that would protect us from them.

While the term "sociopath" often invokes images of cannibalistic mass murderers or savagely brutal criminals, such predators represent only the most extreme manifestations of sociopathy. People with sociopathic tendencies don't typically wind up in prison—in fact, many wind up in the cushioned leather chairs of the executive suite. Most sociopaths remain in the mainstream of society. Some are even considered quite successful. Very few come into direct conflict with the law.

Instead, sociopaths carefully tread the line between legal and illegal—although their journey often takes them beyond the bounds of ethical behavior and fair play. They disregard social convention and norms, which may make them distasteful, but not necessarily jailable.

Jack could be charming to customers. But when he was negotiating with vendors, he was a pretty disgusting man. He occupied much of his day squeezing pennies out of our suppliers.
His favorite trick was to belch loudly when his adversary was
talking. Then he would rub his stomach and say, "Must have
been that crankshaft dealer I gobbled up this morning." He
would lick his lips and make a sour face, and add, "left a bad
taste in my mouth. Now you were saying . . ." Usually the
suppliers would just give in, just to get away from him. Then
he would get the invoice, call them up, and yell that they had
agreed on $1.15 per unit, not $1.23 a unit. I was amazed at
how quickly some just gave in—how they just wouldn't con-
tradict him. But now that I think about it, I'll bet they are still
around and I'm not—I got canned. *(account manager, male,
age 41)*

Sociopaths blame intentional overcharging of customers on acci-
dental bookkeeping errors. They superglue the chrome trim on old
jalopies and hawk them as structurally sound. They conveniently
forget their credit cards when they have invited you to an expensive
lunch. They make fathers grimace when they arrive to take daugh-
ters out for dates. In short, they propel you to keep your hand on
your wallet when they are around.

The sociopath is found everywhere. Unfortunately, this includes
supervisory positions. Sociopathic tendencies are commonly evident in the brutal drill sergeant, the self-righteous and punitive
vice-principal, and the silver-tongued politician. But most sociopaths are found in industry, in business, where opportunities abound
for exploitation and manipulation.

Psychotherapists agree about the unique attitudes and behaviors
that make up the sociopathic constellation. Sociopaths are fearless,
guiltless, and ruthless. They are uncaring, unethical, and uncom-
mitted. They are insincere, irresponsible, and (after their facade has
been cracked) intolerable. But be forewarned, even experts are
sometimes duped by the skilled sociopath.

One telltale characteristic of sociopaths is a glib and superficial
facade. They tell fantastic, yet somehow believable, tales about
their magnified achievements. They will woo and flatter, using their

charm and sense of humor to disarm you. Sociopaths have a gift for saying what you want to hear. They can be smooth and convincing. And before you have a chance to question the veracity of their propaganda, sociopaths will move in for the kill.

> I once had a boss, an oil and gas attorney, who would constantly remind me how good I had it at that firm. I would usually ignore his antics, but when I did stand up for myself, he would become very red-faced and look very intimidating. He acted quite macho, although he was a short man. He walked with a discernable strut, especially after talking to the receptionist. The selection criteria for that position seemed to be how well endowed the applicant was. She was somehow sympathetic to him—she fell for his line about his wife not appreciating him. Anyway, he played her like a fiddle. She bought his tales of tragedy—hook, line, and sinker. Actually, I kind of felt sorry for her. She wasn't that bad, she was just off the farm and very naive. In the end, he broke her heart, and her confidence. After that, she was just useless decoration around the firm. *(legal assistant, female, age 27)*

Sociopaths seek self-gratification at others' expense—taking far more than they ever give. They approach interpersonal relationships as an opportunity to exploit and manipulate. But when they have achieved whatever it was that they wanted from you–be it a sneak peek at your confidential report, a modification of your work schedule, or even a partner in a cover-up—they will discard you like yesterday's *Wall Street Journal.*

Sociopaths have almost no friends, but many acquaintances. They will form temporary alliances if it facilitates their opportunistic schemes. However, they will abandon these alliances once there are no further material gains. Former associates can quickly become adversaries in the face of competition.

Sociopaths operate under the "WIFM (What's In It For Me?) Principle." They won't hesitate if they have to use and abuse you to get what they want. The sociopathic boss views employees as objects—as inanimate, brainless, feelingless objects—that can be manipulated for his or her own purposes.

The ultimate result of this orientation is an unbelievable lack of empathy for others. But this detachment, this emotional bankruptcy, is crucial to the sociopath's persona. The lack of attachment allows the sociopath to emotionally and financially pillage and plunder others without the slightest hint of guilt. While the "normal" person generally has some scruples about lying, cheating, and deceiving, the sociopathic boss is devoid of this moralistic baggage. Rather than worrying about morality, the sociopath is primarily concerned about whether his or her scheme will work.

Sociopaths live in the present—they have little respect for the past and little concern about the future. They don't seem to learn from past mistakes. They don't seem to consider the future consequences of actions. Sociopaths, quite simply, live for the moment. They are impulsive and seek immediate gratification—they do what feels good, what is pleasurable at the time. They are never committed to idealistic goals—though they may profess to be so if it is of utility in achieving their ends. Instead, they seek material gains for themselves.

The only time sociopaths feel remorse is when they get caught being deceitful, and have to expend the energy to weasel out of the accusations. No amount of evidence, interrogation, or proof will induce sociopaths to take responsibility for their aberrant behavior. Sociopaths will not be embarrassed or flustered when caught in a lie. Being trapped in a lie simply presents the sociopath with an opportunity to cover-up, distort, deny, or lie again. Lying, to the sociopath, is an art. And like any art, the more you practice the better you get.

> I didn't like working for Wayne, but it was always interesting. Wayne could do whatever he pleased and get away with it. They rest of us would have been fired 202 infractions ago. I remember one time when Wayne was supposed to drive about two hours up the coast and meet with a client. It was a one-day job, but when his expense report came down, the auditor spotted a hotel room charge—probably got it for some afternoon delight, if you know what I mean. Anyway, the auditor reported it to Mr. Claymore, the Vice President of Operations and clotheshorse extraordinaire. When Mr. Claymore confronted him, Wayne launched into action, explaining that the client had spilled turtle soup down his pants and he needed a

place to wash up and dry his trousers. That was why he got the room. Now who would believe that? But you know, Mr. Claymore did. If Mr. Claymore had been an exercise buff, Wayne probably would have told him he rented the room to do pushups. Needless to say, Wayne was quite convincing. *(computer salesperson, male, age 32)*

Sociopaths have an extreme lack of conscience. In fact, they enjoy and take pride in their manipulations and deceptions. Any appearance to the contrary is simply an act. Their self-presentation style reflects no underlying personal values, but merely the facade they must adopt to effectively and opportunistically take advantage of an audience. What the sociopath hopes to do is seduce and suck in the gullible. And the riskier the scenario, the more attractive it is to the sociopath.

They thrive and seek out dangerous situations and delight in intrigue and mischief. They are bold, daring, and adventurous. A hallmark of sociopaths is their tendency to become easily bored. Routine and monotony are intolerable to sociopaths. Instead, they yearn for excitement, living "in the fast lane" or "on-the-edge." And they are not burdened with anxiety. Calm under pressure, sociopaths are often perplexed about why others experience fear and trepidation. In fact, excessive emotionality is seen as a liability—a disdained sign of weakness.

While I was a navigator, I often flew with Smitty, although I didn't particularly like it. Smitty had been a military aviator and landed a commercial airline piloting job after he was discharged. Funny thing about Smitty, he liked bad weather conditions. You see, they would make him late. Then, as we approached the airport, he would ask for permission to land. Air traffic control would deny and ask him to hold and circle. He would pretend that he couldn't hear them, and land. My God, it was like he was playing chicken with other jets. When we would land, I would be shaken and sweaty, and he would laugh and say, "I had it under control the whole time." When he was reprimanded, Smitty simply confessed that he was trying to keep the on-time landing statistics up. And they were very important to the top brass. The kind of stuff the public looks at. And so he got away with it—I guess he still does. *(navigator, male, age 33)*

The following is a prototypical summary of a classic sociopath.

Bob is an executive director of a mental health center. He is a tall, large, good-looking man in his late forties who has a certain charm and glibness. In his interactions with employees, he is on one hand intimidating in his style and on the other hand somewhat seductive. Thus, workers feel scared of him and attracted to him at the same time. When Bob walks in the room, it is clear that he is to receive special recognition and consideration. His size and booming voice demand attention. When he sits at the conference table, he invariably props his feet on the table and makes a comment on the largeness of his shoes (size thirteen).

Bob seems very proud of being a self-reliant man and has built the largest mental health center in the state. He believes he has accomplished this through his toughness and hard-nosed competitive values. He has had to vehemently fight others who didn't want him in charge of the center, but he took bold risks and won the contracts with the state government.

Upon being granted a state license as a mental health center, he immediately fired two prominent psychiatrists who opposed him, ignoring their threats to sue him. Indeed, Bob has a reputation for dismissing people. His favorite trick is to fire them and require that they have their office cleaned out by the end of the day. Often, these firings occur when he is under pressure from other powerful forces, and it seemed as if these employees were scapegoated.

On one occasion, a female therapist told others that she was receiving obscene calls at home. She said she thought it was Bob who was calling her, but she had no proof. When word of this got back to Bob, he took it to a buddy psychiatrist who suggested that the female therapist was "hysterical, bordering on psychotic breakdown." Bob, skillful in influence tactics, feigned an air of justified innocence. He sympathetically offered the female therapist help through the company's employee assistance program, but she thought it would be wiser for her to leave.

Before becoming an administrator, Bob was a clinician who specialized in hypnosis. Therapists at the mental health center were sure he liked having that kind of power over clients. The grapevine indicated that he was once charged with molesting a female client while she was under hypnosis. These charges were dismissed, however, because of lack of evidence.

Bob has been through several marriages. Rumor has it that he gets quite drunk on occasion. His favorite personal stories have to do with how he used to take off hitchhiking on weekends and the scary adventures that occurred to him on those excursions.

Diagnosing the Defect: Is Your Boss Sociopathic?

YES	NO		
_____	_____	1.	Does your boss feel that what is right is whatever he or she can get away with?
_____	_____	2.	Is your boss a master at worming his or her way out of trouble?
_____	_____	3.	Does your boss react in a forceful, intimidating manner if he or she doesn't get his or her way?
_____	_____	4.	Does your boss often ignore the past when making important decisions?
_____	_____	5.	Does your boss feel that making a profit is more important than doing business honestly?
_____	_____	6.	Does your boss feel that "looking out for number one" is his or her top priority?
_____	_____	7.	Is material gain the overriding source of motivation for your boss?

YES   NO

_____   _____   8. Does your boss brag about manipulating others?

_____   _____   9. Is your boss more concerned about telling you what he or she thinks you want to hear than telling you the truth?

_____   _____   10. Does your boss impulsively take actions without considering the consequences?

If you answered "YES" to more than 7 questions, your boss exhibits strong sociopathic tendencies.

If you answered "YES" to between 4 and 7 questions, your boss exhibits moderate sociopathic tendencies.

PREDICTABLE REACTIONS TO THE PATHOLOGY

Because sociopaths are never bound too tightly to the truth, they can mold themselves to be whatever it is others want them to be. In fact, they are chameleon-like, changing colors as the situation demands. They become skilled at feigning those "natural" feelings that don't come to them instinctively.

Upon first contact, then, the sociopath can be quite appealing. But while you are busy being taken in, the sociopath is studying you. He or she is learning your weaknesses, your soft spots, your frailties. Loaded with this information, you are in prime position to be victimized.

Bob was a large German man with a pretty good sense of humor. His size was intimidating, but his wit put people at ease. I was working as an engineering technician and he was our project team's manager. Before Bob came on board, I had gone through a personal tragedy that required therapy. Since I lived so far out of town, my previous project manager had allowed me to go to therapy during lunch. This meant that once a week I would arrive about thirty minutes after my lunch hour had officially ended. When we had a change of managers, nobody told me to stop therapy, so I continued. Then, after about six weeks, Bob called me in and asked me if there was a problem. I confided in him. He seemed sympathetic and sincere—and allowed me to continue my appointments. He warned me not to say anything about the extra time off—he convinced me that others would be jealous. Then, one day, the vice president approached me in a rage. He said that I had sent an error-filled e-mail message to the production people. When I looked at the message, it had been sent from my account, during a time when I was laying on the couch at my shrink's office. I knew Bob was the only one who would have had access to my password. But I was in quite a bind—either confess about my late lunches or take blame for a problem I didn't create. *(engineering technician, female, age 34)*

Some are repeat victims, falling for the sociopath's con time after time. But others are quicker to detect the true motives of the sociopath. They come to see the boss as cold and heartless, insensitive to feelings, and gaining pleasure from derogating and disgracing others.

Those who insightfully view the sociopathic boss as glib, slick, superficial, and untrustworthy should not expect to be exempt from future exploitations. Instead, when the sociopath's mask is removed, he or she will adopt a less manipulative and more menacing approach. Sociopaths will be forced to resort to bullying tactics in order to get their way. They will employ a forceful and intimidating manner, and their temper may erupt into verbal abuse.

Employees may respond with impotent rage or be provoked into overt anger. However, the sociopathic boss must be thought of as a ticking time bomb with a short fuse. Sociopaths are particularly malicious toward those who appear to have thwarted or mistreated them in some way. When crossed, the sociopath can be a dangerous, vengeful foe, and when he or she lashes out, the sociopath is cold and unemotional—almost impersonal in his or her attack. This impersonality allows the sociopath to feel no guilt about devastating reactions, such as firing employees. It also prevents the sociopath from worrying about what other employees may think about the unfortunate fate of fallen comrades.

Tom is a supervisor of ten security officers at an office building occupied by nearly 200 tenants. He is in his mid-forties and retired from the Navy. To most of his employees, he is intimidating. The tenants seem to love him. So does the main office, because Bob handles problems at the site without getting them involved. One night, he came in to review the work of a new guard. He had obviously been bar-hopping with his Navy buddies. Unfortunately, he was drunk as a skunk, and less than capable of reviewing the guard's actions properly. The guard was fired on the spot for using "nonsanctioned" speech over the radio. He said "Is everything all right on 4?" instead of "All clear on Floor 4?" When I tried to protest, Tom made it quite apparent that I would be the next to go if I didn't keep my mouth shut. So I did. *(security officer, male, age 51)*

Sociopaths express their feelings impulsively and assertively. This may make them appear frank and forthright, but what they enjoy most is shocking and intimidating others. They effectively utilize sarcasm and criticism to frighten others into fearful respect and submission. In fact, some employees may be terrified by their abrupt and bellicose manner.

WHEN THE SOCIOPATHIC BOSS
LOOKS IN THE MIRROR

Most human beings are caught up in the universal struggle of striking a balance between pursuing their own interests and respecting others' rights. When the former takes precedent over the latter, most people appropriately experience some guilt about their selfishness. This guilt strengthens our resolve to become less egocentric and more humanistic.

But no such battle rages in the mind of the sociopath. Instead, sociopathic bosses rationalize their exploitations. They are particularly willing to exploit others who seem successful, because they feel that others are intentionally hoarding and flaunting their riches. Therefore, the sociopath feels justified in taking from those who are perceived to be deliberately and unfairly withholding from them. They are simply claiming what they feel they are entitled to.

The sociopath truly believes and lives by the axiom, "Good guys finish last," while simultaneously rejecting the proverb, "The meek shall inherit the earth." Sociopathic bosses get a high from lying and cheating—in fact, it is more pleasurable to them to scam than it is to work for rewards. Nothing deters them. Sociopaths are masters at coming up with socially acceptable excuses for their deviant behavior, and they adamantly reject blame. Furthermore, they believe that any type of punishment for their behavior is unjustified. They want to be in control, they want to be in charge, and they don't want some pitiful bureaucrat determining their destiny.

The sociopathic boss loves power, yet rejects authority. His or her goal is to be "top dog" or "head honcho" in every situation. The sociopath is willing to exploit others to get to this position, not only to prove his or her superiority, but to enjoy the associated material rewards.

> Richard was an office manager in a utility company when I was under his reign. He was called Dick by those who knew him, and plenty of people did. If one thing made Dick happy, it was the feeling of being in charge. He didn't necessarily like the responsibility that went with being in charge, but he really liked the idea of being in charge. Dick wasn't big on rules and procedures. When he made a mistake, such as when he hired a cocktail waitress that couldn't type for a secretarial position, he worked around his bad judgment by giving her extra evaluation points for her wardrobe. Dick was exceedingly chauvinistic, which was a problem since most of his employees were female. Once he even tried to implement a "no-slacks" rule for female employees. The front office turned him down. But the maddest he ever got was when one of the execs hired an employee and placed her in Dick's department. Being told what to do and who to train was more than he could stand. He went berserk, and eventually forced her to quit. *(troubleshooter, male, age 37)*

From their perspective, "might makes right"—a jungle mentality of sorts where the end always justifies the means. Sociopaths truly believe that their victims get what they deserve and that they were just asking to be exploited. After all, it was the victim who let his or her armor be cracked. The victim placed himself or herself in a weak, compromised position by letting defenses down. To the sociopath, weakness, compassion, humanism, and emotionality are contemptuous. Part of the joy of being victorious is ridiculing the loser. To be ruthless in opportunistic pursuits makes sociopaths feel omnipotent. To them, victory is feeling superior to others, and they cherish rubbing others' noses in their successes. They relish in the humiliation and suffering of their victims.

Sociopathic bosses can't stand for others to be successful. They are unbearably envious of those who have prospered. They desire to displace the successful, and are willing to step on anyone who gets in the way of these pursuits. Beneath their thin veneer of social appropriateness, sociopaths feel no loyalty toward others. They learn to fake feelings of sincerity, but underneath they have no respect for the others' rights or needs. They don't play by the rules of the game, or at least not by society's rules. Instead, sociopaths internalize their own code of conduct, where they are the center of their universe. Their entire value system is crafted around "Looking out for numero uno."

To the sociopath, "numero uno" isn't so bad. In fact, sociopaths see themselves as possessing such admirable traits as being competitive, hard-nosed and no-nonsense, self-reliant, tough, realistic, and strong. In actuality, they are indeed vigorous and energetic, and good in war, love, and athletics.

PRESCRIPTIONS FOR PERSEVERING

Psychotherapists suggest that part of our contempt for sociopaths stems from the fact that deep within ourselves we envy their rejection of repressive rules and societal constraints. Since they don't have to deny or oppress their socially undesirable characteristics like the rest of us, there is often a certainty "honesty" that flows from the lips of sociopaths. To the "normal" population, this may seem quite liberating. But sociopathic tendencies shouldn't be condoned in the workforce. Instead, they should be dealt with as suggested in the following recommendations.

Be Vigilant or Be a Victim

The sociopathic boss is always looking for an easy mark—someone who is ripe for exploitation. Don't let this be you. Sharing stories of personal tragedies or revealing insecurities can provide sociopaths with just the entrée they are looking for. Though sociopathic bosses can appear otherwise, they never develop the capacity for empathy. They will always be competitive and egotistical, never sympathetic and tender. Generally they view employees as gullible, moralistic, and inhibited people who don't know how to win in the workplace.

The sociopathic boss will also be on the lookout for facilitators—individuals who won't expose his or her unethical or questionable business practices. Many employees will be tempted to cooperate, doing anything to avoid the wrath and engender the support of the sociopathic supervisor. But remember, when push comes to shove, the cooperator will likely be left holding the bag, or worse, the smoking gun.

Threats Won't Work

Anticipation of punishment or sanctions does nothing to deter the sociopath's aberrant behavior. Neither does the fear of getting caught. Sociopaths stand unruffled in the face of threats. They will call your bluff, retaliate, or make you question your sanity. Trying to reason with the sociopathic boss will be futile. Instead, you have only two choices—blow the whistle to someone with a higher rank than the sociopath or remain silent.

Don't Try to Teach an Old Dog New Tricks

Trying to change sociopathic bosses is like trying to pull the stripes off a zebra. It can't be done. They don't want to change. Why should they? Sociopaths reap rewards as a result of their questionable behavior. They are satisfied with their lifestyle and exploits. They don't dislike themselves and don't care if others do.

The only sanctuary for employees of sociopathic bosses is Father Time. Sociopathy is likely to manifest by the age of fifteen—starting with minor infractions such as truancy and petty theft. These tendencies then escalate until the sociopath reaches midlife. After that time, there is a decline in overt hostility, and sociopaths will express themselves less flagrantly and publicly. In essence, what happens is that the sociopath (who is three times more likely to be male than female) gets burned out.

Be Neither Friend nor Foe

In the meantime, if you are forced to work for a sociopathic boss, avoid malicious attempts to strike back at him or her. Such direct, punitive approaches don't work. In fact, the boss will get great satisfaction from vindictively doing you in.

On the other hand, don't be ingratiating or try to befriend sociopathic bosses. Friendship is a foreign concept to them, and they will typically not perceive your goodwill as being real. Feelings of social attachment do not fit their perception of the "dog eat dog" world. The best approach is to maintain a respectful distance from the boss. Learn to be tolerant of his or her unattractive traits because he or she is precisely tuned to the subtlest signs of contempt and ridicule. When you have to approach the sociopath, do so from a stance of reason, knowledge, and fairness.

Avoid Three-Martini Lunches

Sociopaths often have problems with substance abuse. This makes them prone to throw back a few at lunch or after work at the local pub. But don't be enticed to accompany the sociopathic boss on these ventures. Sociopaths become more antisocial when they have been drinking. You could be setting yourself up to be scapegoated, victimized, or sexually harassed.

Rick managed the retail store where Marcy and I worked. In just a short while, Rick grew very attached to Marcy. Although she had been working at the store only two and a half months—and others had been there seven and eight years—Rick promoted Marcy to Assistant Manager. At first, she seemed flattered and relieved that someone took notice of her work and believed in her. But then Rick's attention escalated into "advances" that Marcy politely shunned.

Undaunted by rejection, Rick's "friendliness" continued. He commented that he would be the one standing next to her at the altar. He bragged that he owned her and had the employment records to prove it. He would even dedicate songs to her over the radio. The words eventually turned into physical advances—he would put his arm around her waist and hold her arm when he talked to her. He would even sneak into the security room upstairs and just stare at her through the windows. Then Rick started telling other employees about how "hot" Marcy was and how he "wanted her." When she confronted Rick about his comments, he laughed and said her co-workers were just trying to anger her because he held her in such high esteem. He was so good at manipulating that Marcy left his office in tears, feeling guilty for making such ridiculous accusations.

For about a month, all advances stopped. Then, one day when there were no other men in the store, Marcy was forced to ask Rick to help her move a heavy box. He smirked and asked, "What have you done for me lately? What do I get out of it?" She was pensive, until he laughed. After that, the advances resumed—and intensified—until she finally had to quit. *(retail clerk, female, age 24)*

Compensate for the Sociopath's Weaknesses

Sociopathic bosses are not attracted to nor particularly good at performing in highly structured situations. Such confines seem stifling because they have no room for maneuvering, no room for "wheeling and dealing." Instead, sociopaths best use their talents in situations that are in flux—in situations where they can take advantage of others and get a larger share of the pie. If any, this is the saving grace of this shadowy and disreputable character. Negotiating is where they excel. Sales is another. Sociopaths are expert at dumping goods on unsuspecting buyers at high prices. But the tedium of the paperwork afterward is far too boring.

Jane is the co-owner of a small real estate firm in the Southwest. She is a large woman—nearly three hundred pounds—and wears very expensive clothing and jewelry. She is originally from somewhere in New Jersey, where she says "distinguished people come from." Jane has little formal education, but she is a persuasive saleswoman. She seems amicable and informed on the first meeting. But after that? Jane has been married and divorced at least six times according to Harry, her present husband and original owner of the agency. She admits to only three. Before marrying Harry and taking over his business, her primary occupation apparently was "divorce tycoon." It seems Jane has amassed a small fortune in community property settlements. She constantly reminds Harry that she can bankrupt his business and has the track record to prove it, so he passively lets her run the office from her large office and large leather chair. When she wants attention, Jane raises her voice to a high decibelled squeal that reminds me of the famous fingernail and chalkboard torture. What is most annoying is the way she barges in to the middle of negotiations and takes over. It doesn't matter whose deal it is or what the facts are. She will just come in and start talking, and scratching out, and changing all the terms. Then, afterward, she leaves the agents to clean up her mess. *(real estate agent, female, age 28)*

This is where the employee may come in and save the day. Give the sociopath an emotionally charged predicament involving high stakes and he or she will easily exploit the situation. But astute workers should recognize that sociopathic bosses are not good at attending to details. They are also not very good at conceptualizing long-term plans or follow-up. An employee who assumes these (less than exciting) responsibilities will become an asset to the boss—freeing the sociopath to do what he or she does best.

–3–

The Paranoid Boss:
The "You-Don't-Trust-Me-Any-More-Than-I-Trust-You" Type

What loneliness is more lonely than distrust?

George Eliot

DECIPHERING THE DEFECT

The paranoiac's world is fraught with danger. Enemies lurk around the water cooler and threatening messages are written between the lines in memos. Conspirators plot at the back table in the lunchroom and the staff members huddled around the bulletin board are up to no good. To the paranoid boss, peril is just around every corner and behind every door. Paranoiacs suffer from a persecution complex, of sorts. They are convinced everyone, even those who attempt to befriend them, are out to exploit, conquer, and demolish. Paranoid bosses believe the office is a battlefield, and they had better be prepared, for an offensive is imminent. Their modus operandi—attack or risk being attacked.

> When I first interviewed for the position of customer service representative at the optical store, I thought Joan was all right. She seemed a little cautious and reserved, but I thought that might just be good business acumen. But on my first day of work she approached me and told me under no circumstances was I to speak Spanish at work. This seemed ridiculous to me, not because I spoke Spanish (I am unable to speak Spanish), but because the area is primarily Hispanic and some people

35

just naturally converse in their native tongue. I later found out the reason she did not allow employees to speak Spanish was because she thought they might be talking about her and she wanted to know at all times what the employees were saying. *(customer service representative, female, age 36)*

Paranoid bosses can be described as distrustful, intense, cynical, uncompromising, and guarded. Because of their lingering suspiciousness, which is typically unjustified, paranoiacs take precautions against any perceived threat—real or imagined. They infer hidden motives, overreact to slights, and are quick to counterattack. Stubborn and rigid, they almost never relax or let down their guard against possible assault or derogation. They believe that hypervigilance is their key to survival.

Everyone is a potential enemy, so paranoid bosses keep a safe distance from employees and peers. This distance makes interactions with them feel impersonal and cold. They seem void of kindness, sentimentality, and compassion. Paranoid bosses are unemotional and they definitely are deficient when it comes to a sense of humor. To them, the world is not a funny place. On the rare occasion when paranoiacs do show wit, it is usually thinly veiled hostility expressed in a biting and sarcastic manner.

Alice was always so serious—how she ever got a managerial job at a doll manufacturing company I'll never know. We were making dolls, for goodness sake. Wasn't that supposed to be kind of fun? But Alice always reminded us that making dolls was no child's play. Anyway, we really wanted to lighten her up. So on her fifth anniversary with the company, we thought we'd surprise her with a male dancer. We thought it would be funny to have him dress up like a new boy doll we were working on—it was a concept thing—dolls for little boys! Anyway, when she saw him, she was upset. But not for the usual reasons. She was suspicious that he was a spy and might sell our boy doll idea to another company. Let's just say, the prank didn't lighten her up any. *(artistic designer, female, age 26)*

Interpersonal relationships are avoided by paranoiacs. They resist collaborative associations and seem unable to compromise. They refrain from group participation unless they can control and dominate the situation. Paranoiacs abhor sentimentality and withhold empathetic responses, for they believe that if they let their guard down they will become vulnerable. They are often grouchy and testy, displaying grating irritability. In short, paranoiacs are difficult to interact with and are rarely close to people.

Debating or disagreeing with paranoid bosses can be futile. They are convinced that their position is the correct one. Arguments can cause a paranoiac to be hypercritical. They are masters at finding faults and flaws in others. Paranoiacs see others as spiteful and malicious or out to get them. So others are blamed for the paranoiacs' failures. They fear you are out to undermine their efforts or to get them fired.

While the paranoid boss is hypercritical, he or she is simultaneously hypersensitive to being castigated, excluded, or manipulated. The paranoid boss is particularly astute at detecting insincerity, duplicity, and dishonesty. A hallmark of the paranoid boss is that he or she cannot tolerate being in a position of uncertainty or helplessness. To be unsure or confused is far too dangerous in this threatening world. The paranoiac must anticipate all possible persecutory situations. This requires that the paranoiac be secretive, threatening, and unapproachable, all to protect himself or herself.

> Wayne was the comptroller (or should I say "controller") for the company. To be fair, I guess I should say Wayne was dedicated. But he was so dedicated that he wanted complete control over the company's business dealings. He was so concerned in this regard that he often withheld information, which made it difficult to complete projects effectively and efficiently. He would very cautiously share tidbits on what he called a "need-to-know" basis. When he was away from the office, it was very difficult to get anything done because we just didn't have enough information. *(project manager, male, age 52)*

Obviously, each of us attempts to avoid danger. Everyone wants to be protected and feel safe. Hence, it is important to point out that there are varying degrees of paranoia. At the most dysfunctional end of the continuum are the individuals who fear their thoughts are being monitored by television waves beamed straight up to UFOs. These extreme cases represent paranoid schizophrenics who are generally unable to function in the workplace. At the other end, there are everyday paranoiacs who are otherwise normal people whose minds are sometimes clouded by unfounded suspicions. Everyday paranoiacs cringe when they walk into a room and others burst out laughing. "Is it a funny joke, or is it this polka-dotted chiffon skirt I'm wearing?" they wonder. They become distressed when the vice president passes them in the hall and doesn't acknowledge them. They become concerned when they are not appointed to the company picnic committee.

It is difficult in contemporary society to not be at least a little paranoid. Newspapers and television continually bombard us with stories of massive corporate layoffs, asbestos poisonings, fraudulent insurance lawsuits, and ex-employees shooting down former colleagues. Naturally, people worry. Will I be fired? Will there be any money in the Social Security pot by the time I retire? Will I drink too much coffee and develop some obscure type of cancer?

In actuality, though, everyday paranoia isn't necessarily maladaptive. Sometimes it is just good reality testing. Paranoia becomes problematic only when unfounded fears begin to preoccupy one's every thought and action. It becomes problematic when dangers are invented or exaggerated. It becomes problematic when your boss continually questions your loyalty, withholds needed information, or perceives you are out to annihilate himself or herself.

> Sometimes I wasn't sure if it was his office or his fortress. Fred had sealed off access through one door and his desk was positioned tightly against the wall. I was surprised when he could squeeze back into his chair—he wasn't exactly the fit and trim type. In front of his desk was a row of three-drawer file cabinets, which meant if you wanted to see Fred when you spoke to him, you had to stand up. In meetings, he would sit in the corner of the conference room with walls behind him, not at the head of the table where you might expect. He insisted that everything—every drawer, every cabinet, every restroom—be locked at all times. I spent half of my work day looking for the stupid key, so I wasn't exactly productive there. Fred was quick to remind me of how my inefficiencies were letting our competitors get an upper hand.
> *(water purification salesperson, male, age 32)*

Diagnosing the Defect: Is Your Boss Paranoid?

YES	NO		
_____	_____	1.	Does your boss have a pervasive and unwarranted tendency to interpret others' actions as threatening?
_____	_____	2.	Does your boss bear grudges or is he or she extremely unforgiving of insults or slights?
_____	_____	3.	Does your boss unjustifiably question the loyalty and trustworthiness of his or her peers and associates?
_____	_____	4.	Is your boss reluctant to confide in others for fear that shared information may be used against him or her?
_____	_____	5.	Does your boss expect, without cause, to be exploited or harmed by others?
_____	_____	6.	Does your boss overreact and/or counterattack slight insults?
_____	_____	7.	Is your boss consumed with pronounced jealousy or envy?
_____	_____	8.	Is your boss cold, distant, and suspicious?
_____	_____	9.	Does your boss read hidden meanings into benign remarks or actions?
_____	_____	10.	Is your boss preoccupied with the "injustices" of the world?

If you answered "YES" to more than 7 questions, your boss exhibits strong paranoiac tendencies.

If you answered "YES" to between 4 and 7 questions, your boss exhibits moderate paranoiac tendencies.

PREDICTABLE REACTIONS TO THE PATHOLOGY

The paranoid boss is like the human manifestation of Fort Knox. It is impossible to break through the impenetrable walls of isolation the paranoiac builds around himself or herself. Those walls are his or her defense. And no matter how hard you try, it seems there is no way to win the paranoid boss's trust or confidence. The paranoid boss never believes an employee is loyal, and his or her antagonistic, disparaging demeanor precipitates anger, frustration, exasperation, and fear in employees.

In more extreme situations, paranoid bosses may go beyond just questioning employees' loyalty to defaming their integrity. They hold lengthy interrogations concerning employee theft and embezzlement. They harass staff members about information leaks. They closely monitor expense accounts. The paranoiac's suspicions and hostility provoke feelings of discomfort and resentment in the employee. It is as though the employee is falsely accused, and the accuser is judge, jury, and prosecutor.

> My first boss at the chemical company was named Mr. Eisenberg, but we called him Mr. Iceberg. He was cold and ruthless. I always thought he would have made a good prison guard. He would stare at you with his X-ray eyes until you wanted to admit that you had done something wrong, even if you hadn't, just to break his penetrating stare. I remember one business trip where I charged a call to my wife on the company's phone credit card. I didn't mean to. I just punched their code in automatically. I was going to pay for the call, but before I got my copy of the bill, Mr. Iceberg got his. He stormed into my office and yelled that villains like me were the downfall of American competitiveness. How he got there, I'll never know. *(chemical analyst, male, age 33)*

Paranoid bosses misconstrue and overreact almost instinctively. When disturbed, adrenalin starts pumping and they lose their capacity to critically evaluate situations. They make "mountains out of molehills" and those who stand in their way are susceptible to being trampled. The paranoid boss's unpredictability engenders uneasiness. The office becomes tense and anxiety-filled. Because the boss never relaxes, the employees can't either. Working for a paranoid boss is like working in a pressure cooker—never knowing when the boiling point might be reached.

> I knew when I went to work for a Department of Defense contractor that they were going to expect a certain level of discreetness. But I wasn't prepared for Mr. Peruth. To him, everything was top secret—not just blueprints, but even things like office supply catalogues. I think he wished that he could have things magically typed up so I wouldn't be able to lay my eyes on them. It was quite a dilemma for him, but I couldn't even understand half the things I transcribed. I don't know if it was the industry that made him so weird or if it was just his personality. But he was weird. I would sometimes hear him on the phone telling people, "No, I'm not busy, I'm just battling demons." And that is what he really thought. *(receptionist, female, age 28)*

Because the paranoiac makes so many (potentially devastating) misattributions, employees soon learn the best way to deal with the boss is not to deal with him or her at all. They become secretive, just like the boss, and reluctant to disclose any negative information. In essence, the employees become gatekeepers, letting only certain information flow up the communication channel. The problem is, this distance only fuels the paranoiac's fire. The paranoid boss is very astute and will quickly detect being excluded and circumvented. This reinforces the paranoiac's perception that the staff is plotting and conspiring.

The only solace for the paranoiac is within himself or herself. Paranoid bosses have an excessive need to be independent and self-sufficient. They earnestly avoid and seriously rebel against outside influences and control. Since they fear domination, paranoiacs don't like others to be in power. Because they are wary of authority, the paranoid boss is likely to have problems with his or her boss.

> Soon after I began work at the optical store, I noticed that Joan was constantly talking about the general manager. She talked about how he was lazy and took advantage of her. She said he

didn't deserve that position, that she did. She would talk about the other employees with their co-workers. Once I found out she had been talking about me. She snorted, said I was just being paranoid, and waved me off. *(customer service representative, female, age 36)*

When someone has power over them, the paranoiac's feelings of self-reliance are threatened. They avoid cooperation and obligations because they don't want to be seduced into being submissive to another's requests. They will do almost anything to avoid loss of self-control, autonomy, and independence. A common defensive technique paranoiacs use is to be argumentative. They counterattack those in power to avoid being vulnerable to others and to avert feelings of helplessness or incompetence.

Those working for a paranoid boss may not be easily convinced, but the paranoiac may offer a few strengths to the organization. They have a natural talent for ferreting out incongruities in all situations, are particularly skilled in understanding legalistic details, and can develop strategic plans under conditions of complex and contradictory information. Because of their perpetual vigilance, paranoiacs have a knack for detecting threats and challenges in the environment. They are always prepared for emergencies and develop contingency plans for their contingency plans. Finally, they pay close attention to details.

WHEN THE PARANOID BOSS LOOKS IN THE MIRROR

Paranoiacs perceive themselves as lonely hunters whose job is to track down and stamp out the many injustices in the world. It is the paranoiac's mission to expose hypocrisy and wrongdoing wherever it hides. They can never be intimidated, coerced, or seduced into submission by the misguided, naïve masses. They are the honest ones, the insightful ones, who cannot be silenced. They insist on speaking the truth, no matter how painful, repulsive, controversial, or downright unpopular.

Paranoiacs see themselves as courageous hunters, fearless and bold in a terribly malicious and treacherous world. They nobly fight for the restoration of moral order. Because they have undertaken this awesome task, they feel superior to others who they feel are too stupid or too blind to sense the pervasive evil. This is the universe of the paranoiac. The threats are everywhere—they must not only be guarded against, they must be eliminated.

In their struggle, the paranoiac believes the end always justifies the means. Those who attempt to stand in the way of fighting injustices are cowards, or even traitors, who represent evil forces. Because they pursue a higher moral cause, paranoiacs give themselves permission to engage in cruel mistreatment of others. In the secret underworld of paranoiacs, they are relentless superheros in the perpetual battle over good and evil. They will take whatever steps are necessary to win the war.

When paranoiacs learn that others object to their tactics, they are often surprised. They perceive this criticism as a personal attack against them, launched by those who are envious of their moral superiority or who wish to prevent them from protecting themselves. Thus, they feel unjustly treated and oppressed. It is the evilness and stupidity of others that drives paranoiacs to be aggressive. They are innocent and unfortunate victims. They believe they are the underdogs of the world and are shocked that others might perceive their crusades as unreasonable, contentious, and antagonistic.

Whereas the rest of the world may see paranoiacs as social, religious, or political zealots, they see themselves as defiant and isolated rebels searching for the truth. And they find it yet another miscarriage of justice that they are so harshly judged. In this world of intrigue and conspiracies, paranoid bosses see themselves as the primary victims. They simply desire to protect themselves.

Paranoiacs pride themselves on being rational and objective. Yet, they distort reality through the use of "projection." Projection allows the paranoid boss to superimpose his or her thoughts and feelings onto another person. For example, paranoid bosses are often consumed with jealousy, yet they will misinterpret their feelings and become convinced that others are envious of them. Paranoiacs are suspicious of you, but project that you are suspicious of them. That way, they have an excuse, a motive, for their suspicions.

They have, in their minds, a rational basis for lashing out against others.

Paranoid bosses need power in order to control and they need to control in order to ensure their safety and security. When they are not in charge, they are dependent and in a position to be scapegoated. Paranoiacs fear vulnerability. They will mask such feelings because to expose weaknesses would give others an upper hand. Therefore, the paranoiac try to conceal uncertainty, anxiety, and stress. They bluff their way through danger by acting fearless, aloof, and potentially vengeful.

Paranoiacs must be self-reliant. They feel they don't need anyone to survive in this cold world. Alone, they can overcome any impediment, any obstacle, any setback. These tendencies toward omnipotence translate into an air of invincibility. But when the paranoiac's self-confidence is threatened, he or she attacks.

Because paranoiacs mistrust sharing their doubts and insecurities with others, their misperceptions are never corrected. There is never an opportunity to disconfirm their imagined threats and fantasies of doom. So they become increasingly unable to see the world as others do. They use their imaginations, suspicions, and weak evidence to weave an intricate web of deceit and deception. They magnify, they distort, and they invent detriment.

PRESCRIPTIONS FOR PERSEVERING

When the ancient Greeks first coined the term "paranoia," it was simply interpreted as a catch-all word for all forms of insanity. We now have a better understanding of the character of the paranoiac, and that insight leads to suggestions on how to best deal with this type of pathology.

Be a Trustmonger

Since paranoiacs are so suspicious, employees must be absolutely trustworthy. They have to convince the paranoid boss that they will not betray him or her under any circumstances. But rising above suspicion in the paranoiac's eyes will not necessarily be easy.

Trust is developed very slowly and it can be lost very quickly. Paranoiacs play their cards close to their chest and usually refuse to deal you in. The paranoid boss's theme song is not "You and Me Against the World"—it's "Me Against You and the World."

> On one occasion, I was ill and unable to report to work at the jewelry store. Sam called me that morning every fifteen minutes. After about seven calls, I finally told him I could not possibly make it in that day, although I thought it would be funny if I went in and regurgitated all over the diamond broaches. Well, he got furious. He accused me of taking the day off so I could go to another jewelry store and warn them about our Mother's Day sale. It was ridiculous. Every jewelry store has a Mother's Day sale. That is not exactly an industry secret. *(salesperson, female, age 21)*

Since every human being, even paranoiacs, yearn for some contact, the paranoid boss may enlist an employee (or two or three, at the most) in uncovering the intrigues and mysteries of the organization. This is a privileged position, but a tenuous one. Remember, the one closest to the paranoid boss is likely to be the first to sway in the wind when fantasies run amuck.

If you find yourself in a position to bend your paranoid boss's ear, recognize that what he or she cherishes most is someone who will recognize and admire his or her identity as a rebellious, solitary individual on a lifelong quest for exoneration. Also, try to serve as a liaison between the paranoid boss and what is unfamiliar to him or her. Familiarity may breed contempt, but it also breeds trust. Paranoiacs are particularly suspicious of those who are different or unfamiliar. In fact, they are often both ethnocentric and xenophobic.

Don't Try to Prove the Paranoiac Wrong

The paranoiac's world is full of dichotomies—me versus them; good versus evil; right versus wrong; win versus lose. There is only black and white, no gray. So when paranoiacs make a decision, no amount of persuading, reasoning, or begging will convince them to change their minds. Paranoiacs are uncompromising. They approach each negotiation as a win-lose proposition and they will relentlessly strive to be the winner. Arguing with paranoiacs will only make you more suspect.

> Journalists are trained to be skeptical, to look at problems from different angles, to never commit until all the options have been considered—it is an occupational hazard. But Claire apparently didn't realize this. She was the News Editor and my direct supervisor. Claire didn't circulate much, but when she did come out on the floor, she had a clear purpose. She would march up to you, present her idea (or directive), and ask "Friend or foe?" This essentially meant, "Are you going to support me on this or not?" It was a yes or no choice. There was not time for clarification or modification, which essentially meant there was no choice at all. "Friend" was the only answer if you wanted to keep reporting at that newspaper. *(reporter, male, age 41)*

Directly challenging the beliefs of the paranoid boss may expose the insecurities underlying their facade of hostility. They definitely do not want to appear weak or dependent. In fact, they despise others who are too quick to expose their own dependencies. In the paranoiac's eyes, those who are too humanistic are seen as somehow defective. Frailty is disdained by the paranoiac.

Don't Prove the Paranoiac Right

Because the voices of employees are never heard, some may be provoked into aggressiveness. But a belligerent offensive will get you nowhere with the paranoid boss. It will simply make you the prime target of a counterattack. Aggressiveness should even be avoided as a defensive posture. Although you may find yourself the victim of an unprovoked assault, open hostility will simply confirm the paranoid boss's suspicions about your trustworthiness. There are few options, but those available should be consistently followed. Always be punctual, avoid the perception that you are plotting against the boss, distance yourself from threatening information, and always act as an ally to the paranoid boss.

The Truth, the Whole Truth, and Nothing but the Truth

Rigorous honesty is an absolute requirement when communicating with the paranoid boss. Paranoiacs are unusually cunning in detecting even small amounts of truth-bending. They are trained experts in this domain, like human polygraphs. It is also important that you communicate using rational, objective, or analytical tactics rather than relying on emotional appeal. Be calm, distant, and respectful, and avoid being overly friendly. If you don't come across as genuine, you will become even more suspect.

> Jennifer was one of those sticky sweet types. You know, gooey and dripping with feigned pleasantness. She was actually pretty disgusting, like something right out of a soap opera. Each day when she arrived at work she would poke her head in the foreman's office and wish him a good morning. Then one day she didn't report to work. I later learned she had been "relieved of her duties." I wasn't sorry to see her go, but I was interested in why she had been fired. When I asked my supervisor, he simply said, "Because every morning is not a good morning. Anyone who thinks so should be in an institution, not in my department." After that, I kept my greetings to myself. *(assembler, female, age 37)*

Get Your Story Straight

One ploy used by paranoid bosses is to check (and double-check and triple-check) their sources. Any information they receive from others has to be confirmed. Paranoiacs seek to reduce their exposure and susceptibility to any one individual. This means that the boss may be asking you, and many of your peers, for the same information. This may seem like a waste of time, effort, and resources. It may seem like you are untrustworthy and being browbeaten. But it will happen. The challenge you face is to make sure that everyone tells the same tale, reports the same facts, and gets the story straight.

Presentation of a unified front is absolutely necessary when strategizing for positive changes in the department. This will require some coordination and team building among the members of your department. But the alternative is disastrous. The skilled paranoid boss may practice divide and conquer—turning employees against one another. The paranoiac may make employees suspicious of one another's motives, for some will certainly be taken in by the paranoiac's tales of intrigue. Remember, the paranoid boss's primary motive is to confirm his or her suspicions about others. Don't help him or her do that.

After suffering through the paranoid boss's skepticism and unwarranted attacks, it will be hard not to talk, and to laugh, behind his or her back. When this happens, a self-fulfilling prophecy is created. In fact, therapists often say, "Paranoiacs will eventually be right." Eventually employees will criticize and mock them. But if you do, do it out of the paranoiac's earshot, preferably outside the workplace with people not associated with the company.

The Histrionic Boss:
The "Don't-Worry-About-Being-Bored, I'll-Create-a-Crisis" Type

Human nature is greedy of novelty.

Pliny the Elder

DECIPHERING THE DEFECT

"My ship has finally come in," may be your first thought when the new boss with a histrionic personality disorder enters the scene. Upon initial contact, histrionic bosses have a very charming presentation. They appear gregarious, sophisticated, bold, and destined for success. All you have to do is latch on to this rising star. Much to your pleasure and surprise, the histrionic seems willing for you to do so, especially if you happen to be of the opposite sex. You sigh with relief, remembering all the crazies you have worked for in the past and thank the corporate deities for this timely reprieve. Unfortunately, your blessings will likely be short-lived.

Before elucidating the nuts and bolts of the histrionic personality, a little history of this pathology might be in order. In the days preceding political correctness and sensitivity for all, therapists referred to the histrionic disorder as hysteria. But biologically speaking, only females could become hysterical. The word "hysterical," derived from the Greek language, means "wandering womb." It was believed, in the days before X rays and MRIs, that a woman's womb would sometimes spontaneously detach itself and take a road trip around the body, causing erratic behavior. Given that men are wombless, the term could not be used to describe male actions. In the Renaissance days, the cure for hysteria was bland food and bed rest. Today, the preferable treatment is psychotherapy.

We also now know that despite the fact that women are statistically more prone to becoming histrionic, men are also susceptible to this disorder. In fact, males seem more willing to admit to histrionic tendencies than females—men readily admit to primping and using superficial charm to conquer the work world. So, in 1979, the term was changed in the annals of mental health. Thanks to amateur psychologists and the popular press, the outdated word "hysterical" has taken on divergent meanings ranging from "hilariously funny" to "overly reactive." Histrionics is a fully developed personality disorder that often finds its way into the corridors and conference rooms of corporate America.

When encountering this boss, employees may be mysteriously compelled by some invisible force into the histrionic's web. Histrionics devise this trap because they must make themselves so desirable that no one would want to abandon them, which is their deep-seated fear. It is, therefore, natural to be taken in by histrionics—this is their tour de force. Histrionics freely express their thoughts, have an interesting flair for the dramatic, and seductively draw attention to themselves. They are buoyant, lively, overtalkative, easily excited, flirtatious, and emotionally expressive. They relate absorbing stories complimented by exaggerated gestures.

> Marilou seemed to be our knight (or knightress) in shining armor, coming to rescue us from the monotony created by the wormy bureaucrat who had previously run our section. She was like a whirlwind when she arrived on the scene. You couldn't help noticing her, as she commanded attention with her tales and her tail! Her red and gold suit was a department favorite. Going to lunch with Marilou was always quite an event. She refused to go to any restaurant that followed a policy of "no substitutions," because nothing she ordered was exactly on the menu. She always had special requests. Ranch dressing, but no buttermilk; salad, but no lettuce . . . I'm exaggerating slightly, but not as much as you think. At first,

her antics were amusing. Then, after a while, I have to admit it sort of got old. *(public relations rep, male, age 34)*

Notably, histrionics rely not only on their interpersonal style, but also on their physical appearance to reel you in. Female histrionics will often create carefully crafted combinations of cosmetics, clothes, jewelry, and shoes to make a striking appearance. Sometimes, they will even go overboard, flaunting sexual dress inappropriate to the situation. They will saunter, with a little too much swing in their back end, and will toss around their unnaturally colored hair. In short, women histrionics often create almost a caricature of femininity. Male histrionics are not immune to physical ostentatiousness. They are flamboyant in their color coordination, and they often sport tattoos and dramatic hairstyles.

Stacey was the manager of the clothing store where I worked. She was a short, but cute woman with a "bob" haircut. She has a bubbly and kind look, but underneath she is ruthless. When Stacey walked into the store, she had this fantasy that everyone was staring at her and admiring her beauty. Stacey dressed very stylishly, but underneath it all, she really wasn't anything to look at twice. All of us salesgirls would really get annoyed at how she would shake her bottom extra hard when she would walk by male customers. *(retail sales, female, age 21)*

Often attractive, histrionics will use their appeal to govern others. They have such charms that employees will likely idealize the histrionic boss upon first contact. This perception is reinforced by the histrionic's efforts to shower employees with attention and feigned affection. Employees become infatuated and begin to fantasize about meeting the boss's every desire. One's first gut reaction is to reciprocate the generosity the boss is showing. This is the way histrionic bosses "earn" your submission, through their charming enticement and seductive manipulation. In short, histrionics use their social graces to gain the support, nurturance, and acceptance they literally crave.

Another telltale sign of this personality disorder is that histrionics crave excitement. They are allergic to boredom—the mundane and the routine are intolerable. Even the stability that most of us would consider to be comfortable is not within the histrionic's zone of acceptability. He or she longs for and seeks constant stimulation, in both interpersonal relationships and professional activities. This makes the histrionic appear fickle, shallow-minded, and impetuous. Like a chameleon, histrionics can change the color of their spots to fit the situation, which makes them look somewhat flighty. And, they can become quiet distraught over minor irritations. It doesn't take them long to become irrational and throw temper tantrums, especially since they are prone toward jealousy and malice.

> Spiro (his real name was William, but he didn't like it) was always bored. No matter how busy things were, no matter how behind we were, he was bored. He had the attention span of a two-year-old, and he knew it. I am not sure it was possible to keep this man entertained. He always complained that the job lacked challenge. The truth was he did not know the job well enough to determine if it was challenging or not. To keep himself occupied, he would make up elaborate stories about the clients—this one was from Rio de Janeiro or that one had won the lottery and killed her husband. If you didn't play along, or if you tried to ignore him, Spiro's feelings would be hurt. Then you would have to make it up to him or spend the rest of the day hearing him sigh and pout. *(legal assistant, male, age 26)*

Histrionics are likely to overreact and exaggerate when recounting their view of an event. In fact, they are quite capable of lies, deceit, and manipulation. Molehills miraculously turn into mountains, and campfires into blazing infernos. Histrionics are highly affected—indeed, even theatrical. They have such a flair for drama, that you begin to wonder if the office is a movie set and your boss is a third-rate actor performing in a bad B-flick based on a Harlequin Romance. If you were eating popcorn, it would be enough to nauseate you. The only problem is, you can't get up and walk out of the theater. There is no "mute" button. It's like an all-night movie marathon in an unpenetrable prison.

Histrionic bosses can sometimes be dangerously uninhibited when making decisions, especially important ones. Their never-ending quest for adventure compels them head first into impulsively taking reckless courses of action. Rather than relying on analysis and hard-and-fast data, they prefer to go with their gut feelings. Hunches and impressions dictate. Thus, their decision-making style is unreflective. Careful reflection is, quite simply, too tedious. Because they like to be at the pulse of the action, histrionic bosses don't delegate well. In fact, they aren't even interested in input about decisions. They use a quick-and-dirty, no guts-no glory decision-making style.

> The worst boss I ever had? Well, that would be Marsha. I say she is the worst because she and I were so different. She seemed more concerned with seeing her name in the newspaper than with the success of her business. I remember the year when the "season" ended and she realized she would be absent from the social column. Well, she was reading the classifieds, saw an ad for a trampoline distributorship, and signed us up. How ridiculous! We were primarily in the business of distributing spices. Where was the synergy there? When I asked her she said people who used spices were carefree, just the type to buy trampolines. It was ridiculous, but the story was covered in the business section. I had to get out of there before Marsha ran her business into the ground. *(office manager, female, age 57)*

To those with any experience in business at all, it is obvious that some of the histrionic's impulsive decisions are, at the very least, questionable. One likely error is for histrionics to take on new projects, new products, or new lines of business that just don't fit. Their criterion is to be flamboyant, to seek attention. They don't care if employees don't have the necessary skills. They don't care if their action puts the organization in a compromised or conflicting position. Decisions are made for the sake of adventure and for the thrill of the moment, not for the ultimate end. What happens after the chips fall is someone else's concern.

Finally, histrionics desire and need attention. Despite their charm, they are not really interested in others, except for what those others can do for them. Histrionics ravenously consume affection, and once they emotionally drain you, they search frantically for a new source of admiration. They are not in relationships for the long haul. To histrionics, partnering is not a give-and-take deal. Histrionics fear that if they get too close, too personal, others may see through their superficial facade. Not even the histrionic knows, or wants to know, what is beneath the flashy exterior.

Histrionics crave attention and will seek to get it through whatever means possible. Through practice, they have learned that honey catches more flies than vinegar. While at first the boss may appear captivating, he or she later seems shallow and trite. Emotions seem feigned—simply displayed to get attention. Histrionics lack depth and their emotional lability can throw you off keel. They are neither capable of nor willing to hide their feelings. One moment they are enthusiastic, the next they vacillate to boredom. The histrionics' emotions and their attention spans are fleeting. They prefer the insulation that comes from less intimate relationships—here one minute, gone the next.

Diagnosing the Defect: Is Your Boss Histrionic?

YES   NO

_____   _____   1. Is your boss overly dramatic, expressing emotions in an exaggerated manner?

_____   _____   2. Does your boss flit from one relationship to the next, seemingly unable to have a long-term relationship?

_____   _____   3. Does your boss seem addicted to the need for constant attention?

_____   _____   4. Is your boss overly concerned with his or her physical appearance and sexual attractiveness?

_____   _____   5. Does your boss seem scatterbrained, finding it hard to concentrate on any one project?

_____   _____   6. Does your boss often make impulsive decisions, relying on hunches rather than critical thinking?

YES   NO

——————   ——————   7. Does your boss run hot and cold, vacillating between paying you too much attention and then ignoring you completely?

——————   ——————   8. Does your boss make a very good first impression, but eventually is seen as vain and superficial?

——————   ——————   9. Is your boss highly susceptible to physical complaints and illnesses of unknown origin?

——————   ——————   10. Does your boss act seductively, seeming to prefer employees of the opposite sex?

If you answered "YES" to more than 7 questions, your boss exhibits strong histrionic tendencies.

If you answered "YES" to between 4 and 7 questions, your boss exhibits moderate histrionic tendencies.

PREDICTABLE REACTIONS TO THE PATHOLOGY

Many of the characteristics demonstrated by histrionics are those that society, and the business world, value. They are socially adept, relentless in their search for new opportunities, carefully groomed, and, at least temporarily, beguiling. But underneath, histrionics desperately pursue attention and love. It is like an addiction for them. The problem is that histrionics lack depth, so it is hard for them to maintain the favorable first impressions most people have of them. Their sophistication fades into amateurish antics, their sociability becomes promiscuity, and their thin veneer of style is soon shattered. At first histrionic bosses seem trusting, charming, agreeable, accommodating, zealous, cordial, cheerful, playful, and spontaneous, but eventually employees recognize that these bosses are manipulative, demanding, self-centered, emotionally labile, attention seeking, vain, and overly dependent upon others.

Relationships with histrionics are shallow and lack permanence. They constantly seek your attention and approval, but no matter how hard the employee tries, the histrionic's need for admiration never seems to be satiated. As soon as they have sucked you dry, histrionic bosses will turn to another to fill their bottomless pit of needs. They are incapable of having satisfying long-term relationships with others because they lack the internal emotional resources to meaningfully engage in an alliance. Although it is easy for them to form relationships, they quickly become demanding, self-indulgent, and thoughtless. Constancy and predictability are boring for them. Histrionics tend to have a long string of fleeting relationships, especially with members of the opposite sex.

> It is really none of my business—after all, she is just my boss. But I have never seen anything like it. She dates like there is no tomorrow—every night there is someone new. Odds are, at some point, she will find someone to stick with. But it never seems to happen. I often think she needs to join one of those dating clubs—you know, where you fill out a survey and they try to match you up with someone compatible. She isn't doing so well on her own. *(real estate agent, female, age 27)*

Eventually employees come to recognize that they are being played like a fiddle. The coy and seductive chase confuses employees, because the histrionic remains inaccessible. The boss seduces them in and then betrays and abandons them for others. Histrionics are, in fact, stereotypical "teasers," who typically prefer the hunt to the actual feast. They become apprehensive and aloof when their victims want to take their flirtatious behavior a step or two further. This fuels much hostility and contempt in the workplace.

To mitigate this hostility, histrionics are likely to develop psychosomatic problems. They will use these symptoms to attract the attention that they so desperately need. One of their favorite illnesses is laryngitis, which allows them to use dramatic gestures to communicate and also requires the complete attention of others who try to understand them. Sickness not only spices up things, it also allows the histrionic to go to a physician, where attention is almost guaranteed.

WHEN THE HISTRIONIC BOSS
LOOKS IN THE MIRROR

The sad thing about histrionics is that they are not acting. They are as needy, as superficial, as pathetic as they seem. The problem faced by histrionics is that they totally derive their self-image from others. They have no self-identity beyond what is provided to them. When histrionics are asked in psychotherapy how they perceive themselves, they describe themselves only in terms of how others see them. They have no insight beyond that.

So it makes sense then that histrionics are in constant need of attention and admiration. They seek it out with ravenous determination, almost frenzy-like. As soon as it appears someone is about to see through them, they instantaneously direct their affections elsewhere. This leads to emotional deprivation and instability in relationships. It also makes the histrionic appear easily distractible and scatterbrained.

> Joy reminds me of my childhood friend who lived next door. We were close. But every now and then, like when someone new moved into the neighborhood, she would drop me like a hot potato. Joy is sort of the same way. To her, I am the old standby. Not as exciting as she would like, but dependable. I cover for her, give her ideas, keep her nose to the grindstone, and yes, even compliment her. She likes that and she needs that. But Joy doesn't even remember my name when someone new walks through the personnel door. She has to be the first to meet anyone and she likes to think of herself as the "official, unofficial company hostess." Whatever! She always comes back when she starts grating on others' nerves. *(actuary, female, age 62)*

Although we all seek stimulation, reinforcement, and attention at times, histrionic bosses pursue them continually. Their need for recognition and notice seems never to be satisfied, and they will use their seductive charms indiscriminately upon unimportant others in inappropriate situations. These actions are taken to fill a void in their persona. Histrionics must get all of their emotional nourishment from those around them. Thus, to meet their needs, they must manipulate others in their environment.

If they don't get the praise they hope for, histrionics feel anxious and depressed. Lack of positive responses from others is perceived as rejection. Then their life becomes empty and unsatisfying. Therefore, histrionic bosses have learned to become very adept at changing to adapt to the environment. They become what others want them to be. They are very sensitive and tuned into the thoughts, actions, and reactions of others. If you are important to them at the time, they are very aware of your moods. This is particularly true if the histrionic fears impending rejection.

Histrionic bosses generally lack self-insight and they like to avoid troublesome thoughts, thus, they avoid introspection. Histrionics are focused on others instead of their own inner thoughts and feelings. They especially don't like to recognize their dependency needs, although they are prevalent. Even when they are at home alone in the still of the night, histrionics never attempt to get in touch with their true persona. That would be too threatening, too dangerous. What if an introspection of the real self uncovered inadequacies? No, the real self remains a mystery to all involved.

With passing years, histrionics lose some of their natural ability to attract others. They are so vain and preoccupied with external appearances, aging is a very difficult process for them. As histrionics approach their forties, they are likely to feel very anxious and depressed, fearing they will be less desirable to members of the opposite sex, who are their mainstay of attention. During this period, histrionics often treat those of the same sex in a cold, competitive manner fearing competition and envy over their past successes.

> Madeline was a corporate fashion consultant who would come periodically to the stores to check our displays. We all dreaded her arrival. She never complimented us. In fact, she always had to be the center of attention, but she was supposed to be there to help us. Madeline seemed to like tossing all the folded sweaters or jeans on the floor. It was always my feeling that she reacted most negatively to the displays she liked. Weird, but I think she may have been jealous of the attractive designs

she hadn't created. Everyone was afraid of doing anything new or creative because she wouldn't hesitate to chew you out. *(sales consultant, male, age 30)*

Histrionics don't recognize their distrust of others of the same sex. They see themselves as noncompetitive beings who take pleasure in the happiness of others. They believe that they are reliable, credible, and sincere individuals who have others' welfare at heart. They see themselves as gregarious, friendly, and gracious people who should be appreciated for their goodwill. When they find out that others see them as having a hidden agenda of seduction and abandonment, they feel unappreciated, stunned, and injured. Loneliness is one of their greatest fears. This, in part, explains why they reject others so quickly. They would rather be the rejector than the rejectee.

PRESCRIPTIONS FOR PERSEVERING

Be the Histrionic's Right Brain

Histrionics may be dangerously uninhibited. Their world is one of hunches, intuitions, and vaguely formed impressions instead of facts or data. Critical thinking is not their forte. Cognitively, they are flighty, even scattered in their thoughts. Histrionics are highly susceptible to distractions and not too interested in details. They lack the childlike curiosity that can lead to creative solutions. In short, they are intellectually evasive.

Minnie was the supervisor of reservation sales. She was young, average-looking, and overendowed. She liked to wear her dresses tight, and she knew the difference between a virgin daiquiri and a B-52. Minnie wanted to be everyone's friend. She portrayed herself as easygoing and laid back. But you didn't want to cross her. You had to play along. When Minnie had to go to meetings, she dreaded it. When she would take a seat, she would plop her smiling face and chest on the table and ask when the meeting would be over so she could get some real work done. Minnie was more of a PR type than a supervisor. Eventually she left. Some say she was asked to leave. Others say she moved to corporate headquarters. *(reservation agent, female, age 32)*

As a result, the histrionic's decisions are likely to be disjointed. Projects undertaken are often incompatible with the status quo, yet they are disguised under the label "bold." When in strategic positions, diversification into unrelated ventures is a hallmark. Decisions are often made impulsively because they are more dramatic that way. But since they aren't well thought out, the organization may ultimately suffer.

Help your histrionic boss to see that such moves may indeed draw attention, but the attention is likely to be negative. Balance their superficial cognitive style, which is short-sighted and hedonistic, with a calm, objective approach. This should help discourage many erroneous decisions.

Don't Just Jump on the Bandwagon

The histrionic boss is impressionable and responsive to fads. Quick to show enthusiasm, he or she rapidly becomes disinterested. Don't get caught up in the excitement of a new management philosophy or an innovative production technique. Carefully examine the advantages, but don't be blinded to the disadvantages of fleeting fads. Step back from the spur of the moment, or you might be left holding the empty bag.

Don't Get Tangled in the Web

Through being socially gregarious and exhibitionistic, the histrionic boss seeks attention, acceptance, approval, praise, and reassurance. But don't be naive regarding his or her seductive behavior. It is important that employees not become entangled in the histrionic's web of intrigue and deceit. However, it is equally important that the boss be made to feel "special," as he or she feels helpless when others are disinterested. It is also helpful to remember that the histrionic boss is very sensitive to the moods of the employees in the immediate environment.

Don't Get Crushed (In Either Sense of the Word)

These bosses like to think of themselves as princesses/princes who are searching for their princes/princesses. Because others can't live up to their fantasies for romantic bliss, histrionic bosses are likely to become fascinated by those who are unavailable or who remain emotionally distant. By being infatuated with someone he or she hardly knows, the histronic boss is able to keep up the romantic illusion that no real person could possibly attain. Seductive game-playing will only feed into the boss's problem of overreliance on romantic love. Gossiping with the boss may be initially titillating, but has the danger of eventually degenerating into malicious rumors that too directly express the boss's underlying jealousy and rivalry.

> Jana was the manager of the grocery store where I worked. She was twenty-eight and shockingly beautiful. Only she knew it, and she used it to her advantage. She would date the other store managers (who were all male) to figure out what they were doing better and pick their brains about her problems. After a while, they caught on and accused her of "idea plagiarism." Another colleague accused her of sexual harassment and became the laughingstock of the store. But the matter was serious. I knew Jana could be quite vindictive. It was always all about her, never about anybody else. *(produce supervisor, male, age 37)*

Recognize That Sometimes Histrionics Fit the Bill

Although histrionic bosses may not be suited for the long haul, remember their uncanny ability to make a positive first impression. This is one of their strengths, so use it when you can. They have lots of energy that can create momentum for a start-up project. They have a style that can revitalize firms that are sluggish. They like to turn work into play and they can make it seem fun and appealing.

Be the Calm in the Middle of the Storm

Histrionics don't mind a crisis. In fact, they relish the deviation from the routine. As an employee of a histrionic boss, carefully monitor the situation. Look for the brewing storm and when you see it coming, take cover. Make sure you are protected in times of crisis, and then, if you have the resources left, try to protect your histrionic boss. This will earn you, at least for a brief time, a renewed shower of attention.

SECTION TWO:
CONTROLLING BOSSES

Although change induced by threat, manipulation, or sanction may be effective in the short run, it will usually be achieved at the cost of resentment and hostility toward the person dictating the terms.

Sidney M. Jourard

–5–

The Authoritarian Boss:
The "My-Way-or-the-Highway" Type

You do not lead by hitting people over the head—that's assault, not leadership.

Dwight D. Eisenhower

DECIPHERING THE DEFECT

The authoritarian boss is a bully in a business suit. And just like bullies on the playground, authoritarians often end up "king of the hill" in the work world. Authoritarianism is management by tyranny, or management by terror. The authoritarian is a finger-pointing, fist-pounding, fear-inspiring control freak. His or her favorite motivational phrase is "do it because I said so," and when you do, only expect to hear from the authoritarian if you screw up. Authoritarians expect, they demand, total obedience and submission.

The authoritarian boss's undesirable traits go beyond just domineering to dogmatic. He or she is "old-fashioned" (in the negative sense of the term), holding tightly onto very traditional beliefs. They rigidly adhere to conventional values and abhor deviants. They tend to be opinionated and close-minded. Authoritarian bosses are rigid and inflexible in how they see the world. They are often patriotic, fundamental in their religious beliefs, unsophisticated, and antidemocratic. They are ethnocentric so they are prone to prejudicial thinking and the stereotyping of others. In addition, authoritarians are hostile, distrustful, cynical, sarcastic, and vindictive. In short, they are not an enlightened role model for the diverse and participative workforce of today.

Steve was promoted to Staff Sergeant in a U.S. Army Military Police company. Soon after Steve was assigned to my platoon as

65

squad leader, things started to go downhill. Before Steve arrived, we were very tight-knit, to say the least. We had been together for eighteen months without a single personnel change. We had lived, eaten, and worked together, sometimes for months out in the field. Because he was an elitist, Steve drove a wedge between the two squads in the platoon. He constantly created competitions, which began to tear us apart. He was also racist. Within two months after coming to the platoon, all minorities but one noncommissioned officer had been removed. He invented a variety of reasons, but they were all truly invented. *(military police officer, male, age 26)*

Authoritarianism is one of the most reviled concepts in modern management, but it has long captured the fascination of researchers. Interest in authoritarianism first arose when post-World War II psychologists were trying to understand what attracted masses of Europeans to the concept of fascism. Why were these people willing to lay down their lives for such a flawed philosophy? Recently, some interesting insights on authoritarianism have emerged from the strangest place—from those little indestructible "black boxes" that house voice recorders in the cockpit of airplanes.

Investigations of plane crashes have revealed that, in many cases, the copilot suspected there was a problem with the flight long before the pilot detected one. But these apprehensive copilots never strongly voiced their concerns. They hinted at them, they alluded to them, they meekly brought them up, but they were never insistent, never demanding. Again, researchers asked "Why?" Why were these copilots willing to crash and burn, to make the ultimate sacrifice, to risk their lives and the lives of the passengers and crew?

A disturbing answer began to materialize. In several cases, the pilot was perceived as so authoritarian that, even in an emergency situation, "underlings" were unwilling to challenge their superiors. Indeed, authoritarianism can be a dangerous personality flaw.

Authoritarian bosses are quite conservative in their attitudes, seeing only one correct and appropriate way to do things. They cling to traditional ways and have greater resistance to change than normal bosses. At work, authoritarians see clear rank and station differences between individuals. Their behavior and demeanor toward top management is obedient, compliant, and subservient. Authority is accepted as absolute. If another in a higher power position says something is so, then it is so. To this personality type, authority figures are omnipotent and must be obeyed without question or criticism. On the other hand, authoritarian bosses demand the same blind servility from their subordinates.

> My boss, PeeWee, in an on-site CPA for a rental car agency. From the moment he was hired, he went out of his way to make sure he was unpopular with the staff. The only one he respected was the owner of the agency. Many times, he took my work and presented it to the owner as his own. Finally, I had enough. I told the owner it was my diligence that had found the error in intercity corporate billing. When PeeWee found out, he was furious. He lectured me on teamwork and said I must learn to respect him. I told him that if he wanted my respect, he would have to give me his. This boiled him over. That sorry excuse for a man turned to me and said, "No ma'am, I don't have to respect you. I'm your boss." I turned to him and said, "Not anymore!" *(bookkeeper, female, age 29)*

There are places for authoritarians. If you are a prosecuting attorney trying a drug dealer, it would be great to have one in the jury box. If you are at war, it would be great to have one commanding the platoon. If you are a prison guard, it would be great to have one as the warden. But in the participatory, team-oriented culture most businesses are trying to foster today, the authoritarian fits in like a square peg in a round hole.

Diagnosing the Defect: Is Your Boss Authoritarian?

YES	NO		
_____	_____	1.	Does your boss rigidly adhere to conventional and traditional values?
_____	_____	2.	Does your boss seem to distinctly classify employees into one of two camps—either the "in-group," which is treated with respect and dignity, or the "out-group," which is treated with disdain and hostility?

_____ _____	3. Does your boss fiercely lash out against those who violate his or her expectations, values, or norms?
_____ _____	4. Does your boss treat higher-ups with the utmost respect and compliance?
_____ _____	5. Does your boss refuse to question or reexamine his or her decisions?
_____ _____	6. Is your boss racist in his or her orientation?
_____ _____	7. Does your boss have a great deal of trouble dealing with diversity in the workplace?
_____ _____	8. Is it almost impossible for your boss to be open-minded about new ways to approach problems?
_____ _____	9. Is your boss strongly opinionated?
_____ _____	10. Does your boss refuse to have his or her authority questioned?

If you answered "YES" to more than 7 questions, your boss exhibits strong authoritarian tendencies.

If you answered "YES" to between 4 and 7 questions, your boss exhibits moderate authoritarian tendencies.

PREDICTABLE REACTIONS TO THE PATHOLOGY

The authoritarian style is straightforward. Be servile to those with power over you. Dominate and exploit those over whom you have power. Cut and dried. Plain and simple. Some employees can deal with this. Some thrive in authoritarian cultures, preferring the rigid structure and dogmatism to having to make decisions and take initiatives on their own (yes, indeed, there is such a thing as a defective employee). Some truly like executing orders. After all, it doesn't take much brain matter.

As degrading as it seems, such toadies are likely to reap rewards for their toadiness. You see, the authoritarian boss never takes a middle-of-the-road position toward employees. They are either for you or against you. Those who hold the same moral values and see life the same way as the authoritarian boss are likely to be "in." Those who don't (the larger group) will be "out." Again, cut and dried. To be relegated to the "out-group" is a miserable fate. Out-groupers are supervised through coercion and discipline. They are likely to be scapegoated, undermined, and generally hassled by the authoritarian boss.

> JR was a tall, thin lady who supervised about ten probation officers. She had been in the penal system for eighteen years and had worked her way up the ladder. She liked her position, and used it to "keep us down." For example, she had to sign our motions to revoke probation before we could turn them into the district attorney. But, she made a point to turn all motions away the first time we brought them to her. At first, I felt worthless because I could not get one right the first time. Then, I was enlightened by other officers who had been there for years and had the same problem. Even when the motions were perfectly correct, she found some nonsense to refuse to sign them. JR was just showing us her domineering spirit. The same was true the time she wrote me up for coming in early to get my paperwork done! If you grovelled at her feet, you could be late. If you didn't, you couldn't even be early. *(probation officer, male, age 32)*

The authoritarian believes that those in the out-group (which is going to include most employees) are lazy incompetents who intentionally try to incur the boss's wrath, to ruffle his or her feathers. Authoritarian bosses think that people inherently dislike work—a "Theory X" perspective. They believe that employees will not be productive unless it is demanded of them. Essentially, they conclude that most employees are unmotivated and want to avoid responsibility. Thus, to get them to work, the boss must be directive, controlling, and coercive. So the authoritarian clamps down, closely supervises, and readily threatens these "renegades."

Joe is the owner of the car wash where I spent the worst summer of my life. He and I had a different philosophy. I would try to treat all employees and customers with the same respect as I would like them to treat me. But Joe always made it seem as if I was wrong to do so. I assume he expected me to favor people as he did. Because of Joe's attitude, the employees were always intimidated by him. If he wasn't making employees feel dumb, he was embarrassing them in front of customers. Everyone walked on pins and needles around Joe, because, if they slipped just once, he would threaten to fire them. *(car care specialist, male, age 24)*

This effectively eliminates all the internal motivation of employees. Morale becomes nonexistent and employees become subsumed with the idea of getting back at the boss—at exacting revenge. So, the workplace is transformed into a battlefield where tit-for-tat becomes the modus operandi.

Employees become uncooperative, consciously withholding effort and lowering their productivity. Some begin to "work to the rules," doing no more or no less than is strictly required to keep their job. Others will purposely make mistakes or "accidentally" misinterpret the boss's commandments. Some more actively sabotage projects. In essence, an ongoing struggle for control is commenced. It is basically a contest of wills, where only the strongest survive.

Because the authoritarian has used dominance as a lifelong adaptation strategy, he or she is likely to be much more skilled at this unhealthy game than are the employees. For example, the authoritarian knows there is power in numbers. So to prevent the employees from ganging together for a coordinated attack, the boss will try to pit workers against each other. The boss might call you in and say "I thought you ought to know Jim was in here complaining about your work." Soon after your departure, the boss will call in Jim and tell him the same thing about you. Such antics serve to disunify the workers' unified front. The idea is to divide and conquer, and remain stalwart and supreme.

WHEN THE AUTHORITARIAN BOSS
LOOKS IN THE MIRROR

Authoritarians were not born they way they are. It takes much role-modeling and practice to become so autocratic. The authoritarian boss likely had a father who was dominant, distant, stern, and threatening. Their mothers were likely inhibited and submissive. In the household, discussions were not permitted. Signs of disobedience were crushed with harsh discipline. The child soon learned that the parents were right—always. Respect for authority, the importance of work, and the preservation of traditions are strongly emphasized in "authoritarian" families.

> Mark is a Domestic Operations Manager of an oilfield service corporation. He is thirty-four and fairly short at 5′4″. Unfortunately, his lack of stature and his obnoxious personality qualify him for the label "Napoleon." He does have a Napoleonic complex and is proud of his alias. He loves to be hated. And he is. Mark's lack of sensitivity has cost the company thousands of dollars in liability suits. Most of them involve women. He openly says, "Women are harassed because they put themselves in those situations. Harassment suits are just a way for women to get money without working for it." But his hatred of people goes beyond just women. He doesn't seem to like anyone who has worked for him before. In fact, he doesn't even treat them like people. If he isn't being sarcastic, he is cynical and patronizing. If you ask him a question about retooling, he might say, "Well, kiddy, first, you take out the instruction book and learn what the machine is for . . ." And so on. *(machinist, female, age 34)*

Because authoritarian bosses may have had to personally endure unjustified chastisement, they take sadistic pleasure in punishing others who deviate from their expectations of appropriate behavior. The dominant-submissive theme entrenched in their early childhood is carried into their adult working life. Hierarchies, authority, status, policies, procedures, and rules are sacred. Authoritarian bosses see their job as making decisions and ensuring that they are carried out by employees. Empowerment, delegation, and participation are not included in the authoritarian's vocabulary. In fact, authoritarian bosses are preoccupied, or even outright obsessed, with dominance and power. They exaggerate their own strength and overestimate the value of toughness.

Authoritarians have a limited and narrow perception of what is right and just. They are intolerant of differences among people, and they travel in very confined circles. They don't want to learn about those who are unlike them. They simply want those who are different to become like them. If the authoritarian's conventional values are violated by others, they tend to be punitive and rejecting.

> Frank is the president of a large manufacturing company. He could be described as an intelligent, level-headed man until you get on his hit list. Once, we traveled out of town to a trade show. Frank, myself, and two other sales reps went. The other reps were sort of goofy and never really did a good job. At the showroom, a potential customer came to our booth and started asking questions. The other reps offered the man preferential payment options, something only Frank himself thought he should do. So he fired them on the spot. When we got back to the office, Frank called me in to ask what I thought of his terminations. I said I approved. I did. I thought they were losers. But then he started his bad habit of telling one of his war stories. Of course, you had to sit there and listen. But it had been a long trip and I wanted to go home. So I excused myself and left. Sure enough, I was on his hit list then. *(sales rep, male, age 37).*

PRESCRIPTIONS FOR PERSEVERING

Remember, Authoritarianism Is Catching

> I had finally had enough of it. My boss, the regional manager, was constantly on my back. This is wrong. That is wrong. Are you dumb? Why can't you do it how I want it? So I jerked out my pad and I started writing demerits. No one was exempt. I ran out of ink in one of my pens before I had finished. I was

not going to be the only one to take the blame. No way! Then, like a possessed troll, I started handing out the demerits. My employees were shocked. You should have seen the looks on their faces. And the scary part is, I kind of enjoyed it. Until I went home and told my wife. She said something like, the nut doesn't fall far from the tree. I realized she was right. I was acting just like him. *(retail manager, male, age 33)*

An authoritarian is quite capable of turning even the most rational worker into the spitting image of himself or herself. The authoritarian thrives on this and rewards employees for it. Working for an authoritarian can force you to respond emotionally instead of cognitively, which is a natural reaction when you need to protect yourself. The danger is that you may become as constricted and egocentric, as demanding and domineering as the boss. History shows us this happens again and again. After a while, it may even be difficult to recognize authoritarianism as a defect. Take a step back, list the things you don't like about the boss, and make sure you are not becoming the same way.

Authoritarians Have No Allies

In a moment of humanism, the authoritarian boss may actually seem like a real person. But this digression will not last long. Don't be deceived. Comply with the boss's wishes, but keep your distance. Minimize involvement, lest you are willing to sacrifice your soul. The boss doesn't want to be your friend, and the more you expose yourself, the more likely you are to reveal something the boss will condemn you for.

My boss, Justin, prided himself on the fact that people were afraid of him. Well, almost everyone. The only employees he didn't act like a dictator around were those who were like him—uneducated and narrow-minded. He paid these types top salaries—to purchase their souls, I always thought. And these people were close to him. But that was a scary position to be in, because you never knew what you might do or say to turn Justin against you. *(insurance adjuster, female, age 35)*

Don't Try to Undo What the Boss Has Done

The authoritarian is known for making hasty decisions with very limited input from others. But once the decision is made, there is no going back. Authoritarians are always highly confident that they have made the right decision, the best decision. Ambiguity, waffling, and indecisiveness are not tolerated by the authoritarian.

> There were several times at faculty meetings where I voiced my opinion. But Charles, the principal, told me in no uncertain terms that my opinions did not count nor qualify as valuable input. Oh! After that, I began to find it hard to work in a place where my ideas were never heard. *(teacher, female, age 31)*

Just Give In

Those who seek peaceful coexistence with their authoritarian boss should try to be ingratiating. Do what the boss expects, when he or she expects it, and do it well. Don't offer creative alternatives or innovative options. They will not be heard. They will only serve to anger the boss.

It Can't Last Forever

In the long run, authoritarians will self-destruct. Great empires, strong nations, undefeatable armies, powerful governments, and even profitable corporations have all been elevated and destroyed by authoritarians. Followers can only be tolerant for so long. At some point, an internal civil protest will erupt and the true persona of the authoritarian will be exposed. There are many cases where employees have outlasted their authoritarian bosses. It could happen to you!

– 6 –

The Obsessive-Compulsive Boss: The "I'm-Sure-You-Can't-Do-It, But-I-Want-It-Perfect" Type

The desire for perfection is the worst disease that ever afflicted the human mind.

Fontanes

DECIPHERING THE DEFECT

Those who view workaholism as a virtue would argue that a chapter on obsessive-compulsive bosses doesn't belong in a book about defective bosses. In the modern business world, compulsive traits such as perfectionism, conscientiousness, frugality, and acquiescence are often valued. Compulsives tend to be productive and achievement-oriented, rendering them potentially valuable members of business as well as of society in general. But as with most things in life, too much of a good thing can be bad. When there is too much rigidity, compulsivity becomes a disorder.

Compulsives seek the support and comfort, indeed the rewards, associated with conformity. They are overcompliant, oversubmissive, and overly careful about stepping over the line. Compulsives abhor the idea of making a mistake, for mistakes are typically followed by some punitive action and castigation is unacceptable. Bosses with this personality disorder mold themselves into what they believe is expected of "good" employees. They are so orderly that there is a little enjoyment left in their existence. For compulsives, even play becomes work and all the joy one normally experiences in life vanishes. Their inflexibility and overconscientiousness constricts emotions, until they become almost robotic. Everything is done matter-of-factly.

Louise and I were sort of the organizational odd couple. She was neat, I was messy. She was always early, I was always late. She would use file folders, I would use piles on my bookshelf. I think I drove her crazy. But our biggest clash was over something else. She was possessed with being perfect. Every "i" had to be dotted just so, every "t" had to be crossed just so. When she read my reports, I felt like she was my grammar school English teacher. Actually, she would have done that job pretty well. I am sure she never got any meaning or content out of my reports because she was too busy grading them. I could have turned in a bomb threat and it would have been okay so long as my punctuation was accurate. The thing that really bothered me was that these reports were just internal. The only people who would ever see them were the employees in the store. Finally, she recommended me for a promotion out of the outlet. I was thrilled, but I am sure she just did it to get rid of me. *(assistant manager of a retail store, female, age 29)*

Interpersonally, compulsives tend to be stubborn and overcontrolling, particularly when things are not progressing according to plan. Compulsives become quite upset when the preestablished routine is disrupted. They also come across as somewhat reserved and cold, or at least stilted, socially clumsy, and uneasy. Personal relationships are not very highly valued by them. Emotionally, they are grave. Their solemnness is reflected in their serious, cheerless facade.

Compulsive bosses prefer to avoid emotional involvement at any cost. They would rather have a polite, superficial, formal conversation, relating from a position of authority rather than equality or friendship. Warmth, kindness, and human emotion are not shared freely, leading to the perception that compulsives are ungiving. Obsessive-compulsive bosses seem stingy in other areas as well. For example, with material objects, they are tight-fisted, almost to the point of greediness.

Obsessive-compulsives are devoted to work and seem unable to enjoy leisure activities of any sort. Productivity is prized above all else. When pleasurable activities do become necessary (such as vacations), they must be attained through hard work, and they must be planned down to the most minute detail—we will eat here, sleep there, and visit these attractions.

We all chuckled to ourselves when Roger was appointed chairman of the station picnic. Of all people. Sure he was good at planning the details. We knew he would have the drinks iced down to the proper temperature and we wouldn't have to eat with spoons like last year when someone forgot to bring forks. But, he wasn't exactly the fun-loving, laid-back type needed to organize a social event. We even joked that he was going to have a breakdown if there were ants wandering around the picnic sight. Well, what happened was worse. It rained on the day of the picnic. Roger was in a panic. There was one thing he had forgotten—an alternative rain sight. It didn't bother the rest of us much. We held our annual volleyball match in the downpour. But Roger was distraught. It was like he thought he was going to be demoted or something because of the showers. I guess it wasn't too sensitive when we told Roger that Mother Nature was out to get him. *(firefighter, male, age 47)*.

Obsessive-compulsive bosses are often carefully dressed and meticulous, yet underneath they feel very self-conscious and insecure. To exert some control on their world, they are persnickety, moralistic, orderly, persevering, and thorough. They are rarely informal or relaxed. They lack spontaneity and are always seriousminded. Notably, compulsives who are somewhat rehearsed in social graces may use humor, but their sarcastic wit is used to express criticism in an acceptable way. Finding fault is a hobby of compulsives, and they don't hesitate to point out others' errors because it promotes their longing for superiority.

Structure, order, and details are the primary concerns of the compulsive. But although they are methodical, compulsives tend to get bogged down in trivial issues. They have trouble developing overall strategies for their area of supervision and their perfectionism forces a focus on details to the exclusion of the "big picture." They are small-minded in their approach to life's problems, and often can't "see the forest for the trees."

The compulsive boss plans every detail and religiously follows company rituals and norms. Policies, procedures, and rules are heavily emphasized. Compliance is a must. To ensure everything progresses according to plan, compulsive bosses tend to resist sharing their power and authority. Decision making is centralized and subordinates are closely supervised. Everything must go according to plan. The only time a compulsive flounders or is indecisive is when there are no applicable rules or precedents in a given situation.

Compulsives tend to have a narrow view of the world. They rarely look outside the walls of their workplace. The entire industry may be ready to collapse, but the compulsive will remain focused on mathematical inaccuracies in the daily audit. The compulsive tries to reduce uncertainty through intensive monitoring and tight controls. Every move is carefully planned. Projects are not boldly undertaken. Instead, they take one small step at a time. Creativity, innovation, and risk-taking are not in the compulsive's reservoir of business knowledge. Because compulsives tend to overthink situations, windows of opportunity slam shut long before the compulsive has thoroughly analyzed the situation. The unfamiliar is approached with panic, hesitancy, and skepticism.

> When Nurse Jenkins was on the ward, she was a real asset to the hospital. She was very careful about following the doctors' orders, and she was very precise when she charted. No one could fault her. There was strict protocol and she followed it better than anyone. The director of nursing took note of her performance and promoted her to a newly created position—Quality Coordinator for Nursing. In the new position she was supposed to circulate throughout the hospital, looking for nurses who were having problems, and then she was supposed to help them. She was a medical troubleshooter of sorts. Her new job was different every day, every hour. Some problems she might handle include medication reactions, out-of-control patients and family members, fire alarm evacuations—that kind of stuff. Well, she was miserable in that job. She was supposed to handle emergencies, but when one occurred, she became immobilized. It was exactly the kind of job she should not have had, because it required some thinking on her feet. She got the job because she was good at doing the opposite, which was following orders. It's a funny place, this hospital. *(registered nurse, female, age 32)*

One of the reasons compulsives become indecisive in the face of ambiguity is that they are afraid to make mistakes. Therefore, decisions are avoided, deferred, or prolonged. They rationalize their hesitancy to commit by claiming it is only prudent to "look before you leap." But the situation is much more severe than even this. Compulsives look, think about leaping, look again, make a study of leaping options, then look again. Leaping doesn't come until way down the line.

To some, compulsives may be perceived as persistent, industrious, orderly, methodical, and efficient. To others, they are simply stubborn, stingy, picayune, unimaginative, inflexible, and lacking spontaneity. To all, there is no denying that compulsives perfectly fit the image of an anal retentive "stuffed shirt."

Diagnosing the Defect: Is Your Boss Obsessive-Compulsive?

YES	NO		
_____	_____	1.	Does your boss pride himself or herself on being a perfectionist?
_____	_____	2.	Is your boss overcontrolling?
_____	_____	3.	Does your boss insist on always following the rules?
_____	_____	4.	When there are no rules or other forms of pre-scribed behavior, does your boss become inde-cisive and postpone decisions?
_____	_____	5.	Is your boss so preoccupied with trivial details that he or she is blinded to the big picture?
_____	_____	6.	Does your boss avoid being spontaneous and/or does he or she criticize others who act on impulse?
_____	_____	7.	Is your boss obsessed with acquiescing to and pleasing his or her boss?
_____	_____	8.	Is conformity and compliance your boss's major prior-ity?

YES   NO

_____   _____   9. Does your boss demonstrate an excessive devotion
                           to work to the exclusion of pleasure?

_____   _____   10. Does your boss seem overly conscientious?

If you answered "YES" to more than 7 questions, your boss exhibits strong obsessive-compulsive tendencies.

If you answered "YES" to between 4 and 7 questions, your boss exhibits moderate obsessive-compulsive tendencies.

PREDICTABLE REACTIONS TO THE PATHOLOGY

How you react to the compulsive boss depends upon how he or she treats you. How the compulsive treats you depends solely upon whether you are higher or lower in the hierarchy. Compulsives see relationships based not on interpersonal factors, but instead on rank and status. To superiors, the compulsive is respectful and ingratiating, almost to the point of nausea. To subordinates, on the other hand, compulsives are authoritarian, condemnatory, and critical. They hide behind rules and procedures and puff up with pride when they can quote them to you. At times, they actually appear pompous arrogant, and self-assured. This mainly occurs when they have an employee handbook in their immediate possession.

Although sensitive to criticism from authority figures, obsessive-compulsive bosses are not particularly compassionate to their employees. Compulsives often appear contemptuous and deprecatory if they feel the employee has violated some policy. If they decide to take retribution against an employee for a disciplinary infraction, they will fall back on organizational policy, and claim, "It's out of my hands. It says right here . . ." This will occur even as other bosses are bending rules to the point of breaking them.

> Henderson had a straight-laced, letter-of-the-law, never-bend-a-rule type demeanor. When he spoke, he was methodical and deliberate, so as not to make an unintentional stutter. He communicated a sense of inflexibility, discouraging any type of

constructive feedback. But the head honchos thought he was heaven-sent. In fact, if I were a head honcho I probably would have thought he was heaven-sent. He played right into their hands. Others say he sucked up, but I don't think so. I think he really and truly wanted to please them, like he was an orphan and they were his adopted foster daddies. My pal, Jed, once said that Henderson was the brass's prostitute, and he was our pimp. I think there is a lot of truth to that. Henderson expected us to be as devoted to him as he was to the brass. We just couldn't do it. *(computer salesperson, male, age 35)*

On the other hand, obsessive-compulsive bosses are highly opinionated and they don't hesitate to inform you of their strong positions on issues they perceive to be of ethical importance. For example, compulsives tend to moralistically intervene in employees' personal problems (e.g., divorce). Generally, compulsives view themselves as dutiful, selfless, faithful, reliable, careful, and trustworthy. They are proud of their unswerving ethicality to the point of being sanctimonious. They are intolerant of those who behave impulsively or frivolously. Such outbursts of emotions are seen as immature and irresponsible. What obsessive-compulsive bosses don't recognize is that they unconsciously wish to engage in such liberating behaviors. But they don't. They repress any desire to deviate from expectations, so compulsives harshly judge and outwardly detest those who do.

Mrs. Bennett would arrive at work at 7:50 a.m. every day and march through the production warehouse and offices to see who was there, even though the shift didn't officially begin until 8:00 a.m. She would continue her patrol until 8:10 a.m., taking note of what time workers arrived. Those who came in later than 8:01 a.m. would have their pay docked. The business had to run like clockwork, which made clock-watchers out of all of us. People began to take every last second of their breaks and lunches so as to deny the company any uncompensated work. She was more like a drill sergeant than a manager. I always wondered if she was worried that someone might be having a more pleasant life than she was. *(lumber worker, male, age 22)*

In short, obsessive-compulsive bosses are overtly compliant but covertly defiant. With superiors, they come across as dedicated and loyal, hoping to win top management's admiration. They want to be thought of as hardworking and conscientious, always looking out for the team rather than for themselves. They look to top management for validation of these beliefs. By doing this, compulsives set themselves up to be taken advantage of by their bosses. But if the superior does capitalize on the compulsive's servility, he or she feels deeply resentful and hurt.

WHEN THE OBSESSIVE-COMPULSIVE BOSS LOOKS IN THE MIRROR

Although obsessive-compulsives conform and comply with expectations in their environment, underneath they are resentful and enraged about the demands placed on them. To prevent their anger from boiling over, they behave in a constricted and rigid manner. Underneath, they crave to act in an independent, autonomous, assertive, and rebellious way, but they are prevented from doing this because they feel very dependent. Like a volcano ready to blow, compulsives feel an intense boiling inside. They control this impending eruption by being overly conforming, obedient, moralistic, legalistic, and pious.

The boss must rigidly follow the rules of the workplace, because these rules protect him or her from the underlying impulses within himself or herself. Obsessive-compulsives feel threatened by deviations because it may allow their anger to burst out, and then others might question their worth. To guard against this, compulsives sacrifice their sense of identity and align themselves with the organization and its power elite. They constantly monitor themselves and their staff to ensure actions are above reproach.

Why is it that compulsives have this obsessive need to be seen as the "good" employee? One theory speculates that compulsive personalities develop when individuals lack the physical, social, or intellectual qualities necessary to be recognized as special or outstanding. In short, they are, or at least perceive they are, ordinary. So to stand out, to be acknowledged, they adopt their "holier than thou" image. It is sort of a manifestation of the "good soldier" syndrome. Compulsives not only avoid rocking the boat, they also volunteer to paddle it. In short, they become immensely dependable paragons of virtue, hoping to get the recognition they so desperately want and feel they deserve.

Deep down in the dark chasms of their soul, obsessive-compulsive bosses feel terribly unappreciated. They live in fear that dreadful events might occur. For example, any time an executive invites them for coffee, they are sure that their discharge is imminent. They privately feel tortured by their self-doubts. And although they often ruminate about their shortcomings, they will seldom mention such insecurities out loud. Publicly, they don't want to be seen as weak or whimpering. A compulsive would be very embarrassed and ashamed if others viewed him or her in this way.

> A health club is not a good place for worriers to work. There are risks—weights could drop on someone's foot, someone could strain his or her back, or trip on the mats in aerobics. Lee, my boss, was sure that something would happen. He was constantly convinced someone was going to overstrain and die from a heart attack. But what really scared him was that the club might be sued, or even worse, shut down. Part of my job was to help people reduce their stress. I was pretty good at it. But I don't think even I could have done anything for Lee. He was too far gone. He was like a rat in a maze, scurrying here and there to make sure things were OK. He would gripe about such deadly hazards as gum wrappers on the floor. But oddly enough, he would overlook more dangerous obstacles, such as how dark it was in the neighborhood behind the gym where members would often jog. *(fitness counselor, male, age 31)*

If through their toil and persistence, compulsives do reach the proverbial pot of gold, they will likely feel depressed. Events such as promotions lose their joy because compulsives fear revenge from others who are envious. They are also very hard on themselves about their shortcomings. They ruminate and obsess about minor and often irrelevant incidents at work. Obsessive-compulsives can be quite self-recriminating.

I never saw anyone beat himself up like Jack. He was his own worst critic. Jack was the Inventory Manager at the auto repair shop where I worked. Sometimes we ran out of parts. It's a small place. We just couldn't stock an infinite number of all parts. Well, I remember one time we ran out of taillight covers for an imported car. Normal procedure was to apologize to the customer and say we would call and look for the part in the area or we would order it. But Jack went to pieces. At first, he said it was all his fault. And then, he blamed the delivery company, and felt bad because he knew that was not appropriate. After the incident, he beat up on himself for days. You would have thought we ran out of life-support equipment and the customer was taking his last breath. He was good at running his department, kept all the invoices straight, and paid the bills on time. But when we didn't have something, he went over the deep end. *(auto repairperson, male, age 38)*

PRESCRIPTIONS FOR PERSEVERING

Rules Were Not Made to Be Broken

Compulsive personalities like rules. They truly do. Rules reduce burdensome ambiguities, they effectively sublimate rebellious impulses, and they provide for a sense of security and accomplishment. Altering rules is never considered. It would, after all, demonstrate flexibility. And, flexibility is a weakness. Compulsives believe one exception would lead to another until, finally, there would be no order left. Anarchy would reign. There would be no structure, no security, no control. So don't ask for, and don't expect, flexibility. Cognitively, compulsive personalities are dogmatic—they stick to schedules, play by the rules of the game, and follow the letter of the law. Compulsives see things in extremes—right or wrong, black or white, good or bad. There is no gray matter. Such a cut-and-dried view of life does tend to simplify things. Most matters become repetitive. Responses are highly predictable, almost to the point of being mechanical. That is one positive. Compulsives will stick to the book, which results in consistent decisions. No one can ever accuse them of favoritism and preferential treatment!

Attend to the Forest

Compulsives like a well-structured workplace where there are few disruptions. The more highly structured and repetitive, the better. They are content with running a "tight ship" in a predictable and unchanging world. To make sure things operate smoothly, the compulsive boss occupies himself or herself with the minutiae, the insignificant details, the precise observance of trivial rules and petty formalities. The boss will get lost in the details of work, then become blinded to the bigger picture, the grand scheme of things. So while the boss is pruning the "trees," you attend to the "forest." Complement the boss's style by paying vigilant attention to the world outside the department. Keep the boss informed of your observations. Serve as the boss's imagination, the boss's left brain. Do things for the boss that he or she is unable to do alone.

Acknowledge Your Subperfection

When the boss attacks you for being less than competent, don't counterattack. Instead, acknowledge that you know the boss is disappointed that you are, well, less than perfect. Remember that although employees may see their boss as hypercritical and overcontrolling—in short, a person almost impossible to please—the boss doesn't see himself or herself that way. Compulsives believe that their faultfinding is developmental for employees—they believe they are passing on valuable hints about how others can become more perfect people. Their sage advice is meant to help employees overcome their deficits and flaws. Obsessive-compulsive bosses believe that they know the right way to do things, and employees should respect their good judgment.

Indeed, the boss actually hopes to gain the gratitude of the employees through these attempts to improve their defects. Instead, the typical response is irritation and exasperation. When this hostility oozes out, the boss will try to make employees feel guilty because, after all, he or she is only trying to help. When employees defy the boss's attempt at guilt induction, the boss feels wounded and misunderstood.

Recognize That Loyalty Is Not a Two-Way Street

Compulsives are very intolerant of disrespect because it vaguely reminds them of their own forbidden impulses. Therefore, it is important to appear publicly loyal. Any attempts at mutiny will tarnish the boss's angelic image. And besides, you aren't likely to receive a sympathetic ear from upper management when you complain about your defective boss. Compulsives will make sure of that. They continuously forge alliances with those in power, giving them organizational favor. Their subservience and alignment with authority relieves them of blame when employees become upset with them. So it is quite possible you may find yourself with nowhere to turn.

Demonstrate That Perfection May Be Overkill

Obsessive-compulsive bosses clearly internalize the philosophy that if something is worth doing, it is worth doing well. But your perception of well ("good enough") is likely to conflict with the boss's perception of well ("perfect"). The challenge you face is convincing the boss that perfection is not always required. This may, however, be easier said than done.

If obsessive-compulsives could overcome their dependency and fear of rejection, many could lead a more autonomous life. Many are capable of being good problem solvers. They often possess a natural ability for critical thinking, and they certainly have the required self-discipline. However, rather than being innovative in their approach to problems, they regress to an existence of avoiding disapproval from superiors. Therefore, it might be worthwhile to demonstrate that sometimes even those in authority can live with a draft, a guesstimate, or a general idea.

Performance Evaluations

Compulsive bosses evaluate you based on your time-proven compliance to rules and formulas. Know this going in. Don't expect to be rewarded for your brilliant suggestion to stimulate creativity through the implementation of flextime. These are not the things the boss expects from you. It's also advisable that you welcome, not oppose, frequent checkups from the boss. While it may be difficult not to grow defensive about the boss's intrusions into your progress, remember that the obsessive-compulsive just can't help ensuring things are working according to plan.

Just Say "No" to Neuroticism

Some obsessive-compulsive bosses walk a thin line between personality disorder and full-blown neuroticism. If your boss becomes overwhelmed, if the stress gets to be too much, he or she may cross over that line. When the tried and true techniques backfire, or if compulsives are forced to face too many unfamiliar situations, you might wind up with a neurotic on your hands.

This neurosis involves recurrent and persistent thoughts, ideas, images, or doubts that are distasteful to the boss. To block out these obsessive thoughts, neurotics may engage in repetitive, purposeful behaviors performed in a ritualistic manner. This is done because the neurotic believes that only through these rituals will danger be eliminated. Common forms of organizational neurosis include: (1) checkers—those who do, check, check again, again check again, and so on; (2) cleaners—those who wash their hands until they are raw and then refuse to touch any doorknobs; (3) hoarders—those who keep meticulous records dating back to the turn of the century; and (4) organizers—those who truly believe a cluttered desk is the sign of a cluttered mind.

Neurotic obsessive-compulsives suffer from the disease of doubt— doubt about how to handle the world around them. From the employee's perspective, though, there should be no doubt. If you work for a severe neurotic, recommend psychotherapy and start packing your desk.

7

The Explosive Boss:
The "I'm-Sorry,-But-I-Can't-Promise-I-Won't-Blow-Up-Again" Type

Come not between the dragon and his wrath.

William Shakespeare

DECIPHERING THE DEFECT

"Ex-Employee Returns to Office and Slays Former Supervisor and Three Employees." "Boss Found Dead in Walk-in Freezer—Disciplined Worker Suspected." "Man Opens Fire on Workplace." Such shocking headlines are becoming all too familiar in this environment of economic stress and heightened job insecurity. Civility is becoming less and less commonplace in the work world. Altercations once reserved for the barroom are now creeping into the boardroom.

Many victims of workplace violence would never have expected it could happen to them. Often these attacks seem unprovoked, unpredictable, and unwarranted. While violently explosive criminals are dealt with by law enforcement, there are many explosives who have worked their way up the organization ladder, but they never quite cross over the line from inappropriate to illegal. Yet the employees who work for explosive bosses are very much victims, as are the pieces of furniture that get broken and the ashtrays and paperweights that get thrown. The only difference is that employees working for these explosive bosses don't have the help of the police. These workers are, instead, left to handle the situation on their own.

The difficulty in diagnosing explosives is that they are not always fire-spitting, towering infernos. In fact, sometimes explosives are downright docile. But the slightest of provocations can transform the calm and peaceful, compliant and passive lamb into a tense and belligerent lion. These frightening outbursts stand in striking contrast to the boss's "normal" behavior. Between these incidents, the explosive boss can be quite friendly, sociable, happy, and amiable.

> I remember one conversation with Rashad that started out friendly enough. Then I said something in passing about his overly conservative budgetary estimates and it was as if someone flipped a switch and turned Rashad on full power. In a matter of about three seconds, he went from reasonable to rabid. I was so shocked, I just stood there. I didn't know what to say. In fact, I still don't know what to say when he blows up. Usually I just try to melt away into the sunset. But it certainly teaches you to watch what you say. I have definitely learned that honesty is NOT the best policy—at least not around here. And that can be dangerous in this line of work. *(nuclear engineer, male, age 32)*

There are three unique things about an explosive's outbursts: (1) they seem totally out of proportion to the event that triggers the tantrum; (2) there is often no sign of aggression, even within seconds prior to the attack; and (3) following the outburst, the explosive will appear quite regretful and repentant. In fact, it is the explosive's proneness to uncontrollable excitability and his or her sudden oversensitivity to environmental pressures that sets the explosive boss apart from other defective bosses.

Explosive outbursts are, in essence, comparable to adult temper tantrums. The exploder is someone who walks around in adult clothing but has the emotional maturity of a two-year-old. When something goes wrong, or something doesn't go his or her way, the most common reaction is rage. When observing an explosive at the height of an outburst, you will have serious doubts about whether or not the boss is under control. The truth is that they barely are. Yet these tantrums become almost an innate response in explosives, much as in infants, when two preconditions are simultaneously fulfilled in the explosive's cosmos. The first precondition is that the explosive must feel pressured to do something and the second condition is that the explosive must feel thwarted and psychologically threatened (although threats may be subtle and unintended). At first, the exploder feels angry. Then, he or she becomes suspicious and blaming. All the while, the object of tantrum is likely to be confused, bewildered, and horrified.

The exploder has not premeditated the unleashing of his or her wrath. The outbursts are unplanned, with a total lack of prior intent. In fact, the tantrum is likely to come as a surprise not only to the victim, but also to exploders. But this just serves to make the exploder all the more scary—they haven't thought through their actions so until they happen, no one can predict what the exploder will do! It is an unscripted frenzy, of sorts. Employees are left with the impossible task of diffusing a time bomb when they don't even know the ticker is armed.

If you would have asked me last year about my least favorite boss, I would have told you about Ben. In reality, there was nothing wrong with Ben, except that he fired me. He said I was a loose cannon. I thought he had a few bolts loose. I didn't understand then, but he fired me because of my outbursts. At times I would just boil over. I didn't see anything wrong with it. And I didn't mean anything by my little displays. But Ben insisted they were bad for morale and productivity. I started thinking about that, and now sometimes when I have an outburst, it is as if I'm floating above, looking down at myself. I don't really know the person I become. But I had better figure it out—before I lose another job. *(lawyer, male, age 42)*

There are some cues, though, that the observant employee may be able to pick up on. Explosives might openly reminisce about some of their minor scrapes with the law (such as bar brawls). The explosive also may be enthralled with weapons and may drive like an Indy 500 racer. But mostly, the employee has to wait for an outburst to recognize the boss's explosive tendencies.

Diagnosing the Defect: Is Your Boss Explosive?

YES   NO

_____   _____   1. Does your boss seem prone to brief but violent outbursts?

_____   _____   2. Does your boss negatively overreact to relatively small incidents?

_____   _____   3. Does your boss seem surprised and remorseful about tantrums at work?

_____   _____   4. Does your boss seem to have just two extreme temperaments—either extremely friendly or extremely aggressive?

_____   _____   5. Does your boss attempt to excuse his or her hostile behavior through apologizing?

_____   _____   6. Do you feel as if you are constantly walking on eggshells while in the presence of your boss?

_____   _____   7. Do you resist being honest at work, fearing the boss's violent reactions?

_____   _____   8. Does your boss seem to blow things out of proportion?

_____   _____   9. Is your boss only able to express himself or herself through ranting and raving?

_____   _____   10. Is your boss overly reactive to criticism or questions about his or her family?

If you answered "YES" to more than 7 questions, your boss exhibits strong explosive tendencies.

If you answered "YES" to between 4 and 7 questions, your boss exhibits moderate explosive tendencies.

PREDICTABLE REACTIONS TO THE PATHOLOGY

Working for an explosive boss is like walking through a crime-ridden, gun-infested neighborhood late at night carrying an unconcealed stack of hundred dollar bills in your hand. You know the attack is coming, but you don't know when. So you never let your guard down. The thing about explosives is that when they sheepishly apologize after one of the unprovoked attacks, they think everything is okay. Explosives are typically oblivious to the devastating and long-term impact of their explosions. Others are truly more aware of how close the boss is to losing it than the boss is.

> Sonny, the warehouse department head for a major beer distributorship, has a great ability to cut costs. At times he is actually tolerable. He can be very friendly and can act very professional and suave. But when things don't go his way, he becomes a raging bull. He starts cussing and yelling and throwing things around. But his anger is usually misdirected. No matter what or who he is mad at, the person that bears the brunt of his anger is the one who is in the nearest vicinity of him. I remember once he used my calculator and discovered someone else's error. He stuck it in my face, about two inches from my eyeballs, then threw MY calculator in the trash. Later I told him to quit yelling at me for someone else's problems. He replied, "I am not yelling at you, I am yelling to you." Either way, the effect on me was the same! *(delivery driver, male, age 35)*

It is difficult to remain openly hostile to the explosive for two reasons. First, you fear stepping over the trip wire that will launch the next attack, and second, between eruptions, the boss doesn't seem so bad. But even if the anger dissipates, the fear doesn't. The explosive's poor (or nonexistent) impulse control is quite unsettling. Not knowing when the boss will take offense, you can never let down your defense. This leaves employees feeling betrayed, confused, and generally helpless.

> I vacillated between despising and pitying Melanie. She could be so mean, so intimidating. But she always reminded me of a

cat whose tail was stuck in the door. She sounded ferocious, but maybe she had cause. The bad part was that you couldn't avoid setting her off. She would react to the tiniest things. Although I wanted to trust her, I was never quite sure when she might spurt out, "You're fired!" I finally had to quit. It was like working on a balloon in the middle of a pin factory. *(stage actress, female, age 26)*

Employees are left wondering, "Why?" Why can't the boss control his or her temper better? Why can't he or she be more reasonable? Why can't these bosses express themselves without yelling at the top of their lungs? In short, you are left considering whether your boss suffers from multiple personality disorder or at least a dual personality disorder. While almost everyone, at some time or another, boils over with rage, explosives take this route more frequently than others. Explosives don't know how to be assertive. Assertiveness is one response along a continuum of possible behaviors individuals use to react to others.

Individuals can be passive and allow their rights to be trampled. At the other end of the extreme, individuals can be aggressive, trampling on the rights of others. But somewhere in between these two dysfunctional responses is the preferred tactic of assertiveness. Assertiveness allows one to express one's position while respecting the position, rights, values, and opinions of others. Explosives do not know how to be assertive. So time passes and their anger builds until they have no choice but to resort to aggression. Then, like a volcano, they explode. But their rage erupts at a level that is inappropriate to the stimuli that set it off.

Aggression involves standing up for personal rights in a way that is often dishonest, usually inappropriate, and always violates the rights of others. Aggression manifests itself when four stimuli are present: (1) the aggressor feels powerless and threatened; (2) the aggressor has permitted his or her rights to be violated in the past and therefore feels an outburst is justified; (3) the aggressor believes the only way to make his or her feelings known is through aggression; and (4) aggression has worked in the past. This explains, although does not excuse, why explosives tend to go ballistic over such small events.

Sally actually owned the home health care business, but we all knew it was her husband, Mike, who really ran things. It put us in a tough spot. Mike would cat around, spying on us. Then he would go to Sally and insist that she do something about the things he didn't like. Word had it that if Sally refused, Mike would have a tantrum. We speculated that the reason she always had new office furniture was because he used it to take out his anger. And I believe it. Sometimes it sounded like a train was passing through Sally's office when Mike was in there. Needless to say, we were all afraid of Mike. *(physical therapist, female, age 31)*

WHEN THE EXPLOSIVE BOSS LOOKS IN THE MIRROR

What separates the men from the boys (the criminalistic sociopaths from the explosives) is that explosives experience guilt. In fact, it is their feelings of guilt and their related need for reassurance and support, that spurs explosives to want to openly talk about their tantrums. Most explosive personalities are genuinely confused about their periodic transformation from Dr. Jekyll to Mr. Hyde. They lack insight into the factors that spur their vicious attacks.

But they are really not all that mysterious. Explosive outbursts simply cover up fears of victimization and vulnerability. Unfortunately, explosives lack self-insight into this process. They just know that outbursts make them feel more in control. In fact, tantrums can make the otherwise defenseless boss empowered. Having a tantrum is like giving a weakling a gun. Tantrums are the great equalizer.

His name was Lee, which rhymes with tea, which might be why we all called him the Teapot. But whatever the reason, the name was fitting. He was just like a teapot—simmering over a low fire. Steam would build up inside him, but you would never know until he started spouting and screeching. When that happened, we all scrambled to turn down the fire, but none of us knew how. We just stood around in his wake, waiting to be scalded. When I would explain the situation to my wife, she would say he was just acting like a baby, so get out of his way. But have you ever seen a 270-pound, 6'4" man throw a tantrum? It is much more ominous than my three-year-old son misbehaving. *(architect, male, age 37)*

In terms of interaction, the explosive personality has the most difficulty with people of the opposite sex, which explains the high incidence of spousal abuse among explosives. Explosives tend to view the other gender in extreme stereotypical terms. For example, male explosive bosses may view the friendly female worker as a harlot, while the aloof female worker will be seen as a snob. This reaction likely occurs because the male boss feels inadequate as a man. To defend against threats to his masculinity, he is likely to engage in "macho" activities such as weightlifting, boxing, reckless driving, and drinking.

PRESCRIPTIONS FOR PERSEVERING

Boost the Explosive's Self-Esteem

Though the employee may perceive the boss as a peevish, demanding abuser who subjects employees to unfeeling treatment, insult could add to the employee's injuries. Perhaps the best rule of thumb for dealing with the explosive boss is to help build his or her self-respect. This internal self-respect, in turn, will help the boss with his or her self-control.

> Elaine, the purchasing manager, once asked me to white-out a phone number on a laminated piece of paper. But, the white-out would not cling to the paper, so I opted to copy the page on the copier, blocking out that particular number. Then I relaminated the new paper. At first Elaine seemed pleased with the results. But after she thought about it for a second, she came unglued. She went on a rampage, cursing me for not doing what I was told. The attack was completely out of context and out of proportion. I suddenly found myself being very defensive. I am still mad at her, even though I have gone on to another job. And I guess it is also important to add that she did later apologize. After looking back on it, I think she was mad

because she did not come up with the idea of recopying the paper herself. *(university receptionist, female, age 23)*

If You Can't Say Something Nice . . .

Explosives are notorious for their intolerance of criticism, even criticism disguised under the helpful notion of "constructive." Criticism is perceived as a threat to the explosive's authority and is likely to trigger an offensive.

Duck During Outbursts

During the explosive boss's outburst, the most important thing is to avoid flying objects. Having retreated to a relatively safe haven, you might want to try to help the explosive regain control. This can be accomplished by interrupting the explosive's tirade through continuously repeating his or her name or neutral phrases such as "Wait a minute." Accompany your words with dramatic physical gestures, such as waving your arms. This might break the explosive's spell of concentration—hopefully before any unforgettable and unforgivable things are said. However, it's important that the boss not feel babied or patronized, because reminding explosives of their feelings of weakness and dependence may result in another destructive outburst.

Once you have the explosive boss's attention, try to break off (or at least postpone) the interaction. Say something like, "I need to take a restroom break," or "I have to make a phone call." Do whatever it takes to let the boss have some private cooling-off time to prevent him or her from (further) embarrassment. Before you leave, promise to return (in fifteen or twenty minutes)—then come back as you promised.

When you do return, let the explosive boss know that you are taking him or her seriously. Say something like, "I am trying to understand." Convince the explosive that your intention is to be supportive. Otherwise, the tantrum may be recycled, as the boss might begin to feel humiliated. Alternatively, you might just passively wait until the explosive settles down. Eventually, even the most persistent explosive will run out of steam.

We all came to expect Jim's antics, but none of us knew how to handle him. He would start yelling, then someone else would start yelling, and soon we would all be yelling and no one would be listening to anyone else. The victor seemed to be the one with the largest lung capacity. Finally, we all got together and decided not to play his game because we couldn't beat him. In fact, we started joking around before staff meeting, reciting our new corporate credo—"We tried to yell, we tried to fight. But now we realize might makes right. So keep you seats and keep your head, otherwise you might get dead." Poetic, don't you think? *(pilot, female, age 34)*

After the Dust Settles

Expect explosive bosses to come scrounging for forgiveness following a tirade. But when they do, don't shower them with attention and affection in an attempt to reconcile the relationship. Letting them off the hook too easy will only reinforce their explosive behavior. Instead, when you confront the boss about the tantrum, use the following three steps: (1) define clearly what you are upset about (e.g., the fact that the boss took a relatively benign comment and blew it out of proportion); (2) describe your feelings (e.g., "When you get so upset, that leaves me feeling . . . "); and (3) describe what you want done (e.g., "If you think I am mistaken, let me know, but I would prefer that instead of getting angry . . ."). You may want to replace the words "getting angry" with "going berserk," but resist that temptation, or risk finding yourself in the headlines!

8

The Passive-Aggressive Boss: The "You-Can't-Make-Me-if-I-Don't-Want-To" Type

Such individuals go through life making enemies instead of friends and constantly blame the other fellow for their short-comings in accomplishment.

Karl Menninger

DECIPHERING THE DEFECT

Those of you who are parents will be familiar with passive-aggression—it is a preferred tactic of determined and defiant children everywhere. The signs are telltale—a sullen stare daring you to make them budge; a sudden and complete failure of memory regarding any standing request you have ever made; and a sheer determination to remain inert in the face of your frustrated pleas. The combination of behaviors is enough to push you over the edge and you can't help wondering, why? Why does my otherwise pleasant and cheerful offspring resort to such nerve-grating tactics? The answer is simple. Children (and unfortunately, sometimes bosses) resort to the power tactics of the powerless. In power struggles where overt aggression would clearly be retaliated against, the passive-aggressor simply becomes obstinate. Stubbornness replaces temper tantrums.

The passive-aggressive boss does not express rage in a loud, emotional, fist-pounding, desk-kicking manner. In fact, the passive-aggressor doesn't express anger openly at all. Instead, feelings of aggression are often communicated covertly through such behaviors as sulking, stubbornness, sullenness, irritability, and obstinacy. This passivity minimizes the risk of rejection or retaliation. Yet, it allows the aggressor to win out, without being viewed as a tyrant. Conspicuous expression of hostility is avoided because the passive-aggressor can't face direct confrontation. He or she hasn't got the stomach, or the nerve, for it. But hidden beneath a placid, dormant facade is a raging reservoir of conflict and bitterness.

> Clifford was pathetic. But I didn't see that at first. During my interview, he seemed quiet, unassuming, and kind in a naíve sort of way. I should have known something was up. He was just too damn nice, never a cross word about anyone or anything. He seemed like the type who would go out of his way to accommodate you. And even after the semester started, I still believed that. No matter what someone asked, he would agree. In fact, after a while, I began to wonder if the word "No" was in his vocabulary. About halfway into the semester, my suspicions were confirmed. Clifford didn't say "no" himself, he just used others to say "no" for him. What he did was blame others for his unwillingness to help me out. I would ask to teach on Monday mornings and he would blame the clerks for changing my schedule to Thursday nights. I would ask to be on Committee A and he would blame another department head for putting me on Committee Z. But if he really wanted to, he could have met my requests. He simply didn't want to. *(professor, female, age 26)*

A passive-aggressive's sublimated hostility usually reflects resentment about not finding gratification in a relationship with someone or something that they are overly dependent upon. This explains why passive-aggressive behavior is so often manifested in the workplace. Employees (except those lucky independently wealthy types) work because they have to. This creates an economic dependence upon employing organizations, as well as upon the higher-ups. Problems arise when passive-aggressives feel they are not appropriately recognized in these unbalanced relationships. Unlike they rest of us, who sometimes take the option to openly protest being unfairly taken advantage of, passive-aggressives fear it is too dangerous or in-effectual to express such an opinion forthrightly.

Instead, they vent through thwarting the efforts of others—espe-cially those that may be contributing to the success of the organiza-tion. So while your boss may be angered about his or her inequita-ble salary, he or she may impede your efforts to do your job. This defense mechanism is known in psychotherapy circles as "displace-ment." Displacement refers to shifting negative feelings about one person or thing to another that is less powerful. Alternatively, pas-sive-aggressive bosses may be impeding you because they are, in fact, angered at you. It is sometimes impossible to tell.

> Although most people look forward to the merriment of the month of December, I dread it. December is the month we all get our performance evaluations. Now I don't really dread them for myself. I dread them for my boss. No matter how he is appraised, he is never pleased. I'm sure he has received good marks, but he always complains that some of his "criti-cal contributions" were overlooked. It's like an old record we play every Christmas season. And the problem is, he takes out his frustration on us. In fact, I'll bet I can guess his rankings; I'll bet they are always a notch or two above what he gives us. How we are evaluated doesn't depend on how we perform. It depends on how he was evaluated. Not much room for cheer and goodwill around here. *(third grade teacher, male, age 36)*

For the subordinate of a passive-aggressive boss, the quagmire is twofold. First, it's difficult to detect if the boss is even mad at all. And second, it's difficult to determine who or what the boss is mad at. It's enough to drive you mad!

Fortunately, passive-aggressive bosses don't typically make it to the pinnacle of organizations. Unfortunately, they often do rise to positions of lower and middle management, despite their bull-headedness, intentional inefficiency, and stalling.

> John seemed to be going places in the company. He was my team leader, and it was obvious the brass wanted to bump him up into an executive position. But they required an MBA for all their administrative jobs. They wanted John to go back to

school and they even offered to pay his tuition and give him some time off if he needed to take a class during the day. I never got a college education myself, but even I could see what a sweet deal they were offering him. They were dangling the brass ring in front of his face. All he had to do was reach out and grab it. But he wouldn't. Semester after semester, John mysteriously seemed to miss the enrollment deadline at the local university. He was unbelievably self-defeating. They held the job open for him for a while. But finally, he was passed over. Now that I look back on it, I think John resented the fact that the company was trying to force him to do something he didn't really want to do. He thought his life experiences should have been enough to get him the promotion. But the company had rules. I think he thought he was going to hurt the company, but he really just hurt himself. *(machinist, male, age 24)*

Besides not performing at expected levels, passive-aggressives avoid doing those extra things around the office that help it to run more smoothly. Don't ask them to substitute for you, to cover for you, or to chip in to meet a deadline. They won't.

Rather, they are often uncooperative and unaccommodating, carry a chip on their shoulders, and seem contemptuous and surly. Passive-aggressives are the type that may say, "we have an open-door policy," but also infer, "so don't accidentally walk in here." They are known for their edgy irritability and social contrariness. They whine and complain. They are moody, discontented, sulky, and generally have a negative disposition. In short, they are malcontented sour pusses that dampen the spirits and pleasures of those around them. Passive-aggressives are also chronic complainers. They often use hypochondriacal symptoms, such as cramps or headaches, to get their way.

I once worked as a jack-of-all-trades at a small dry cleaning store. It was a family-owned business, run by Smitty and his wife, Veronica. Smitty was okay, but I was not sure about Veronica. She seemed to do things in an underhanded way. For instance, we once did business with a chemical sales rep that Veronica didn't like. She tried to convince Smitty to do business with another supplier, but the rep's prices were the best. So on the days when the rep made an appointment, Veronica would stay home claiming to be ill. Then, right before the appointment, she would call Smitty and ask him to come home and take care of her. Her favorite ailment was some gastro-intestinal gobbledygook. It was hard for Smitty to say no, so he would cancel his appointment with the rep. Finally, the rep stopped calling. I'm sure she must have thought Smitty was intentionally avoiding her. *(laborer, male, age 23)*

With employees, passive-aggressive bosses are fussy and demand-ing. They seem to look for the worst in each situation, and are easily annoyed, provoked, and offended by trifles. Thus, in the drop of a hat, they can quickly shift from being agreeable to being negative. But what is most frustrating to the employee of a passive-aggressive boss is that even though more effective behavior is possible, he or she chooses to hold back and resist indirectly.

The arsenal of the passive-aggressive's covert weapons can be summarized in three categories: (1) forgetting, (2) misunderstand-ing, and (3) procrastination.

Forgetting

Instead of simply admitting that he or she doesn't want (or doesn't think it is a good idea) to do something, the passive-aggres-sive will readily concede to requests and suggestions but will quickly "forget" to follow though. Passive-aggressives seem, in fact, to be cursed with a deficient memory—they forget time and time again. After a while, a subordinate's friendly reminders will likely demise into nagging, making the subordinate appear to be the heavy. This turns into a vicious cycle. You ask, the boss forgets, you nag, the boss grows resentful and forgets more stuff. Noticeably, though, passive-aggressives' failing memory is selective. Things that are pleasurable or beneficial are never forgotten.

Misunderstanding

If the passive-aggressive boss does happen to remember that you asked for something, it is very unlikely that he or she will remember correctly. Passive-aggressives have an uncanny inability to get the message straight. Misunderstandings abound, so statements such as "I thought you said you wouldn't need that travel approval till next week," or "I didn't think you would mind me mentioning that job offer you received last week to the vice president" easily flow from the lips of the passive-aggressive. Such snafus are, in effect, a form of payback. A related problem is that passive-aggressives never seem to learn from their mistakes. They will make the same errors again and again, not because they can't improve, but because they secretly don't want to. This kind of passive-aggressive behavior can inspire others to act the same way, such as when the secretary intentionally transposes two digits in an address to undermine the boss's efforts.

Procrastination

A final irksome technique passive-aggressives use is perpetual procrastination. "It's next on my list" or "I'll get to it as soon as I can" are excuses often offered by passive-aggressives. Trying to pin them down is like trying to nail Jell-O to the wall. In the meantime, you will come off as impatient or demanding. When the passive-aggressive boss finally does get around to your project, he or she will be plagued by personal inefficiency, stonewalling your every effort. Similarly, tardiness comes easy to the passive-aggressive. He or she will chronically arrive late for meetings and appointments, with an encyclopedia of creative, if not believable, excuses at his or her fingertips.

> At a general employee meeting last October, the CEO said that the company, bowing to pressure by customers, was going to pursue the ISO 9000 quality certification. At the meeting I was sitting next to Mack, my section head. When the announcement was made, I could hear Mack grumbling under his breath. But during question-and-answer time, he never said a word. I knew the certification would mean additional work for all of us. But I thought the experience would be good, not just for the company, but for me personally. So I volunteered to be on a couple of project committees. A memo was sent out about the meeting times and places. We all got one, including Mack.

Then, predictably, about thirty minutes before my meeting, Mack would miraculously conjure up a critical deadline that would prevent me from attending. For a while, I though it was just dumb luck, bad timing. But after the third or fourth "emergency," I began to wonder. If Mack didn't want me to be on the committees, why didn't he just say so? *(mechanic, male, age 32)*

Passive aggressiveness is often so subtle that you find yourself confused. Is my boss doing this on purpose, or . . . ? For a while, the only way to recognize this personality disorder is the frustration you feel from the needles that quietly and mysteriously end up pricking your back. Recognizing passive-aggressive behavior may take weeks, or even months. And since passive-aggressives can't easily or honestly admit their anger, they will insist your accusations are totally off the mark. In fact, passive-aggressives may be so skilled at sublimating hostility, they themselves may not even realize they are mad.

Diagnosing the Defect: Is Your Boss Passive-Aggressive?

YES	NO		
_____	_____	1.	Do you find yourself agitated at your boss, but can't really point to any specific reason why?
_____	_____	2.	Is your boss Mr. Nice Guy one minute and pouty, sulky, and sullen the next?
_____	_____	3.	Is your boss often late and/or does he or she often procrastinate?
_____	_____	4.	Does your boss too often conveniently forget things that are important to you?
_____	_____	5.	Does your boss repeatedly misunderstand things that are relatively straightforward?
_____	_____	6.	Does your boss covertly display anger or hostility?

YES   NO

_____   _____   7. Does your boss actually seem relieved when things
                           go wrong for you?

_____   _____   8. Does your boss easily become frustrated and obsti-
                           nate?

_____   _____   9. Does your boss make you feel guilty or twist things
                           around to make them your fault when he or she is
                           clearly to blame?

_____   _____   10. Do you often find yourself being stabbed in the back
                           by a boss you believed to be supportive?

If you answered "YES" to more than 7 questions, your boss exhibits strong passive-
aggressive tendencies.

If you answered "YES" to between 4 and 7 questions, your boss exhibits moderate
passive-aggressive tendencies.

PREDICTABLE REACTIONS TO THE PATHOLOGY

There is no denying, rationalizing, or excusing it—passive-
aggressive bosses are frustrating. They have an uncanny ability to
make your blood boil and you won't even know why. It's nothing
big you can really put your finger on, but their attitude is enough to
make you seethe. And just when it looks like you will finally get
exactly what you want from your boss, you actually get less. Promises are broken, hopes are dashed, and goals are thwarted, even after
they agree to support you. The passive-aggressive's quiet manner may
dupe you into believing he or she is a "nice guy" type. You come to
the point, however, where you would actually prefer a boss who is
occasionally unaccommodating, but actually willing to follow through.

Passive-aggressives are proficient in their ability to spread misery.
Not only are passive-aggressives pessimistic about their own lives,
they are similarly dissatisfied with others. Passive-aggressives are keen
faultfinders, grumbling incessantly about the bad ideas of others. They
tend to demoralize the efforts of employees with their discontent,

complaints, and criticisms. And then, they will gripe about the lack of support the receive from staff members while simultaneously berating top management for their lack of sustenance.

The passive-aggressive boss doesn't tune in to what the employee does right, they seek out what the employee does wrong. Passive-aggressives seem to almost enjoy finding fault, undermining, and even obstructing employees efforts. In fact, they seem to rejoice when things turn ugly. No matter how an employee responds to a situation, it seems to be wrong. This leaves the employee feeling on edge, constantly waiting for the silent hatchet to drop. Employees end up walking on eggshells, so as to preserve the passive-aggressive's fragile mental balance. When passive-aggressives are provoked, their brooding and sulking provoke discomforts for all those in the vicinity.

Because they are self-centered, callous, gloomy, disagreeable, irritating, uncooperative, and overdemanding, passive-aggressives predictably tend to be unpopular bosses. They provoke exasperation and anger and after a while, employees simply get tired of their unpredictable moods, negativism, pettiness, general stubbornness, and tendency not to do what others wish. They burn out. But efforts to transfer out of the department are likely to be met with resistance—passive resistance, of course. In fact, you may find yourself buried under an avalanche of guilt. Guilt is what passive-aggressives use to manipulate you and reel you back in. Passive-aggressives can twist things around so that even you end up believing that the boss was well-intentioned and innocent and that he or she is the victim and you are the aggressor. Suddenly, your anger melts into remorse. Then, you may actually feel sorry for him or her!

I had a constant nagging feeling that my boss, Sheila, was never quite pleased with my work. Sometimes she would bark a little at me, sometimes she would just belittle me, and sometimes she would simply clam up. But never a word of encouragement, never any enthusiasm. So when a job vacancy in another department was posted, I asked her to sign my general recommendation form. Sheila seemed shocked that I wanted to leave her area. I hinted at her lack of positive feedback, and she quipped that this wasn't kindergarten where you got a gold star for showing up. She accused me of acting for my own glory and not for the good of the organization. She actually made me feel a little selfish, a little greedy. *(graphic artist, male, age 37)*

The passive-aggressor wears many masks. The martyr, the obstinate, the aggrieved, the angry, the guilt-ridden, the misunderstood, the frail—these are all guises of the passive-aggressive. Uncertainty about how to react to the boss keeps people on edge. What is most unbelievable is that many passive-aggressives don't realize the effect of their frustrating behavior on others.

WHEN THE PASSIVE-AGGRESSIVE BOSS LOOKS IN THE MIRROR

Passive-aggressive bosses generally feel inadequate, nervous, agitated, and depressed. They succumb to their feelings of empty unhappiness about their state in life, often verbalizing that things never seem to go their way. The problem is they project blame for all their internal discomforts onto others. They feel misunderstood and unappreciated. As a result, they are distrustful of the world and are easily discouraged and angered. Passive-aggressives feel deceived, degraded, and even persecuted. Yet they lack insight into how their covert obstinacy causes them difficulties.

I have never been accused of being overly optimistic, but compared to my boss, Cheri, I was a regular Pollyanna. She seemed to live in constant fear that we were going to be victims of "rightsizing"—that at any moment, our department was going to be eliminated from the organizational chart. The irony about this was that we worked in accounting. How can any company afford to completely do away with accounting? It was ridiculous. But to her, it was a real fear. Another ironic thing—believing that our jobs were in jeopardy, you'd think she would have done something. Talk to top management, for instance. But she never did. In fact, the more fearful she got, the sloppier her work became. It seemed to me that this was the time for doing a better job, not a worse one. *(internal auditor, female, age 30)*

Passive-aggressive bosses think the world owes them a living and they blame the world for not providing adequately. They believe they are acutely sensitive individuals who have inappropriately suffered due to others' inconsiderateness, which leads to a pervasive sense of disillusionment. But while they are cynical, discontented, and disenchanted, they recognize their underlying dependency on those around them. This makes them feel powerless.

So passive-aggressives experience a volatile mix of preoccupation with their own failings, inadequacies, and perceptions that they are being taken advantage of. Passive-aggressive bosses consistently resent expectations from employees and may feel anxiety when pressured to perform. The passive-aggressive boss harbors resentment against those with a more optimistic outlook—they denounce such people. They seem to believe that employees have an easier life than they do, so they are critical and cynical of employees' achievements. However, underlying this cynicism, they are green with envy.

To avoid being taken advantage of and misunderstood, passive-aggressives are constantly ambivalent toward others. These bosses will question your loyalty and are afraid of committing or allying themselves with you. Cognitively, they are in a state of turmoil. Their thoughts shift about what is the best thing to do. Finally, they act on the spur of the moment.

Passive-aggressives also tend to be impulsive in terms of their moods. They seem to be lying in wait for something bad to happen. This may make them appear restless, fidgety, and impatient. They are easily offended, and have a low threshold for frustration. Therefore, passive-aggressive bosses can range from being distraught and dependent one second to being stubborn the next. Passive-aggressives vacillate between periods of self-deprecation to lobbing accusations at others. In short, passive-aggressives are ambivalent because they do not know whether to be dependent or independent. So they are, in some respects, both. They avoid jeopardizing those they are dependent upon by independently, yet quietly, undermining their actions.

When I took the job, all of my friends asked me if I was nervous. I guess I should have been—it was a position that you really needed experience to do, and I was just out of school. But I wasn't nervous. I thought it would be a great opportunity to learn the industry. I knew I would make mistakes, but isn't that a natural part of learning? Bette, the human resources director at the company, was my boss. She had been in HR for twenty-seven years. And so I knew she knew the score. Bette had questioned my ability to handle the job, but I didn't mind that. She was right to question my ability. But once I started working, she seemed supportive enough. Bette would approve all my ideas for training programs, which I was very relieved about. She never criticized anything I suggested. I thought, "This job isn't so difficult after all"—until I went in to conduct seminars. I found my topics had already been covered. I also learned that employee surveys had been conducted for suggestions about needed training topics, but I never saw them. I quickly discovered Bette's lack of interference was giving me just enough rope to hang myself. *(training specialist, female, age 31)*

PRESCRIPTIONS FOR PERSEVERING

Be Decisive in the Face of Indecision

Passive-aggressives are ambivalent about everyday life, so they are indecisive and somewhat unpredictable. Interpersonally, they don't know whether to be obedient and dependent on a significant other or to rebel. Nor can they make up their minds about whether to take initiative in the workplace or to wait for someone else to pick up the ball and run with it. And, when something unexpected happens in the work environment, they cannot decide whether to handle it directly or circuitously. Their inability to settle upon one direction leaves employees floundering. Therefore, it is up to the employee to decide what's best and then to do it. It is up to the employee to take the "bull by its horns."

Expect to take over and handle areas that create high anxiety for the passive-aggressive boss, but don't expect to be rewarded for it. In fact, anticipate the opposite. If you seem harmless enough, you might even experience one of the passive-aggressive's brief outbursts of anger. But after the verbal chastisement, expect the boss to feel (or to feign feeling) guilty. Through this self-condemnation, the boss hopes to regain the support and sympathy of the employee. In this circumstance, avoid any sympathetic gestures that may reinforce the childish antics of the passive-aggressive.

Open the Can of Worms

Passive-aggressives may or may not know they are angry. They may or may not be angry at you. If they are simply taking out displaced hostility on you, there is little hope. Alternatively, if the true target of their anger is you, try to bring the boss's hidden hostility and resentment into the open. Find out what it is you do or don't do that signals the passive-aggressive's alarm. Figure out what is making the passive-aggressive angry and then help your boss figure out that he or she is angry and why.

If the passive-aggressive can recognize the hostility, perhaps it can be dealt with aboveboard. But remember, the passive-aggressive will never trust you enough to be honest if he or she thinks you are trying to ignite a power struggle. You must convince the boss that he or she is the one with the authority, that you are not in a position to threaten the boss in any way, and that even if you were, you would never move against the boss.

Remember, the Truth May Set You Free

Assisting the passive-aggressive boss in this soul-searching is not likely to be a pleasant exercise. You want to find out why the boss is angry, but you may not like the answer. Perhaps your deadline was forgotten because he or she didn't like the premise of your project. If this is the case, receptively listen and respond maturely to the boss's efforts at veracity. But remember, changing you plans to appease your boss is the easy part. Finding out what he or she wants changed is more difficult.

Accept No Excuses

Passive-aggressives will predictably drag their feet unless you keep them from doing so. Stay on their heels. Force them to engage in forward motion. This is best accomplished by asking for and providing feedback (so as to eliminate any possible claim of confusion); supplying your boss with a list of your goals and deadlines and what he or she needs to do to assist you; and being ultraclear in any correspondence or communiqués.

Don't Just Do It Yourself

Going through the motions to ensure your boss is on the same page as you are can seem like a grand waste of time. You will likely be tempted to fall into the trap of, "Oh, hell, I'll just handle it myself." But remember, the more the passive-aggressive gets away with his or her dysfunctional behavior, the more it will be reinforced. Additionally, you run the risk of showing the boss that you actually have the power to circumvent him or her. Instead, what you want to do is discourage the boss's obstinacy. Be persistent, but nonthreatening. Take the time and spend the effort to face your boss about his or her concerns, but do so in a noncombative way. Gently, yet insistently, force the boss to do what he or she is paid to do.

Recognize That Passive Aggressiveness Is a Natural Reaction

Passive aggressiveness is sort of an innate, albeit primitive, defense mechanism. Yet, it is a tactic we all resort to at some time. We mutter "Just try to make me," (or something to that effect) more often than we would probably admit. But we do so selectively—only when we can't conjure up a more rational response. The problem with passive-aggressives is that passivity becomes their only response. To eliminate the response, you have to eliminate the source of the problem. Given that the source is stress, of all sorts, this may be difficult in the typical office environment. But to whatever extent you can minimize threats, pressures, and obstacles, do so—for your sanity as well as for what is left of the boss's.

SECTION THREE:
NEUROTIC BOSSES

My being hath been a living death, with a continued torture.

Philip Massinger

9

The Masochistic Boss:
The "Go-Ahead-and-Dump-on-Me,
I-Live-to-Suffer" Type

There is a sort of pleasure in indulging grief.

Thomas Fuller

DECIPHERING THE DEFECT

Any discussion of masochism inevitably arouses fantasies of black leather collars, whips, chains, and other bondage paraphernalia. But for those who work for a masochist, the outlook is not nearly so intriguing. The dictionary defines a masochist as one who derives pleasure from being offended, dominated, or mistreated. The problem with working for a masochist is that although the boss may delight in being the organizational fall guy (or gal), it is very unlikely that others will share the boss's affinity for self-destruction. When the boss willingly becomes the scapegoat, the blame spreads beyond the leader to the whole department.

> You know, I don't care if he wants to take the rap for everything from poor sales to global warming, but it doesn't take a genius to realize that s___ rolls downhill. So it is not just Jerry that begins to stink, it is all of us. And we don't deserve that. *(shoe salesman, male, age 24)*

The mental health profession's accepted term for masochism is self-defeating personality disorder. But a defect by any other name is still a defect. Masochistic, or self-defeating, bosses don't assert themselves. Instead, they wait to be asserted upon. They accommodate, at all costs. In fact, they are very ineffectual at saying "no." They take on more than they can handle, and they are very poor at setting limits. They have an unexplainable urge to do more, to be more, to take more than others even wish to dish out. Excessive volunteer work is one hallmark of the masochist—and they pursue their work with missionary fervor. Their exaggerated, selfless desire to help others may conjure images of altruism. But, they actually seem to find solace in being taken advantage of.

Masochists repeatedly set themselves up for failure. They refuse help when they clearly need it. They avoid activities in which they might succeed. In fact, they seem to be drawn to employment situations where disappointment and defeat are inevitable. And, they make extreme sacrifices although they are not asked, nor expected, to do so. Then, masochists willingly accept blame for their shortcomings. In fact, they are quite skilled at apology. They express their sorrow and remorse openly. In short, they self-berate, self-humiliate, self-sacrifice, self-handicap, and self-sabotage.

> Theresa was a born loser, I think. And she liked it. When things were going well, she did one of two things—she would actively look for something to go wrong, or she would minimize our accomplishments. She would say, "Well, this research really isn't that important in the bigger scheme of things." It was as though she would look right through the silver lining for the black cloud. *(tobacco industry researcher, female, age 37)*

In contrast to themselves, masochists always view others as always more right, better informed, and higher qualified. Many of their sentences begin with statements such as, "I am probably wrong but . . . ." Their overwhelming lack of self-confidence, accompanied by their overwhelming desire to be everything to everyone, sets the masochist up for certain misery.

Masochists seem to feel disappointment, self-doubt, and discouragement throughout their lives. They mistrust and expect rejection from others and often feel lonely and isolated. They do not see themselves as equal to others in their environment, and hence they are openly unhappy. Notably, the masochists does not try to conceal feelings of gloominess. Instead, masochists believe negative affect conveys that they are sensitive, compassionate, and sincere human beings. They also believe that their belittling self-malignment, self-defacement, self-criticalness, and self-blame symbolizes their humanism.

> I was just a tech [technician] at the psychiatric institute, but I picked up things. I watched for patterns, and I saw one in my boss. First, he would take on more work that he could handle. Second, he couldn't finish the work. Third, he would apologize and take full blame for the failure. Fourth, he would hope that those who were mad about the work not being finished would take pity on him and forgive him. It happened like that all the time. Sometimes it worked and sometimes it didn't. Why not just explain in the beginning that he was too overworked already to take on anything new? Why waste all the emotional energy? I guess that was his only chance for getting a little attention. I became convinced that he could use more than one trip to the psychiatrist's couch. *(medical technician, male, age 36)*

When looking toward tomorrow, masochists are anything but hopeful. They live convinced that the future holds nothing but continued pain and suffering. And in some ways, they make sure that happens. Masochists continually fail to take a reasonable course of action so that they can experience humiliation and defeat. Some may actually fear success. Others may just seem unbelievably accident prone. Still others may be pitied as terribly unlucky. But, with all masochists, just when it looks as if things are going their way, they will somehow manage to "snatch defeat from the jaws of victory." This allows the masochist to realize his or her unconscious need to be punished.

> Marti was my boss when I worked at the paper mill. She was nice enough, but she was the type that was always shooting herself in the foot or putting her foot in her mouth. Marti would take unnecessary risks. When production was high, she would speed up the line. Why? The unions were all over her. Injuries occurred. The machinery couldn't take it. Marti created calamity. The brass kept giving her chances. I think they liked her. Or at least they felt sorry for her. But sometimes

it was like she went out of her way to bring their wrath down on her. It was like she wanted to be struck by lightening. *(production worker, male, age 58)*

The key to recognizing masochists is their tendency to "self-handicap." This means the boss takes on so much that he or she cannot possibly get it all done. Masochists try, they labor, and yet they still fail. But what they have done is provide themselves with a built-in excuse—a handicap—a justifiable reason to fail. This way, it is difficult to get completely fed up with the masochist.

> The thing that most infuriated me about Albert was that he never stood up for us. I remember one time everyone in the Local News Department got together and went to talk to him. We were making a lot less than the writers in the other sections. We told him that we wanted him to go talk to the editor and ask for an across-the-board raise of 5 percent for us. We would still be making less than the other reporters, but at least it would be something. Well, my girlfriend is the editor's assistant and she was there when Albert went to ask for the raise. She told me this is what he said "I know in Local we haven't always fully covered the political scene like you wanted, but my reporters need a raise." Well, hell. He gave the editor a perfect excuse to deny us. Can you believe that! It was like he said, "We don't deserve it, but . . ." Of course, we never got the raise. But the darndest thing is that I could never stay mad at him for too long. Albert just seemed so needy, so pathetic. *(newspaper journalist, male, age 29)*

Diagnosing the Defect: Is Your Boss Masochistic?

YES   NO

_____   _____   1. Does your boss have a hard time saying "no," even though he or she has to suffer the consequences?

_____   _____   2. Does your boss share his or her sufferings as if these disclosures are a gift of intimacy?

YES	NO		
_____	_____	3.	Do others' needs or opinion matter more to your boss than his or her own needs?
_____	_____	4.	Is your boss incessantly apologizing, even for things that are not his or her fault?
_____	_____	5.	Do you wind up feeling fatigued and frustrated after attempting to cheer up your boss?
_____	_____	6.	Is your boss his or her own worst critic?
_____	_____	7.	Does your boss allow others to take credit for his or her ideas?
_____	_____	8.	Does your boss seem to feel that happy employees are out of touch with how painful the world is?
_____	_____	9.	Does your boss refuse to stand up for himself or herself?
_____	_____	10.	Does your boss willingly take on excessive work, even when he or she is too busy to handle it?

If you answered "YES" to more than 7 questions, your boss exhibits strong masochistic tendencies.

If you answered "YES" to between 4 and 7 questions, your boss exhibits moderate masochistic tendencies.

PREDICTABLE REACTIONS TO THE PATHOLOGY

When you first encounter masochistic bosses, you might think, "I'm glad I'm not in their shoes." They seem overworked and underappreciated, exploited and abused. Initially, you might even be tempted to jump in and rescue them from drowning in a whirl-pool of projects and paperwork. But much to your surprise, masochistic bosses reject your relief efforts. They insist they can handle it and even take on more. At this point in your relationship, you might be wondering if you have gone to work for Superboss, Ruler of the Corporate Jungle. But your confidence will soon be shattered. The masochistic boss can't live up to your image. Deadlines are missed, promises are broken, sure things go sour, and the smooth-running office falls into disarray. This is when the masochist starts whining. "I tried to do my best, but I guess my best just wasn't good enough." "I thought it would work out, but that is what I get for thinking." "Nobody should trust me; haven't I proven that time and time again?" It is a constant barrage of poor, forlorn me—like stale country music lyrics.

But it is hard to stay mad at the masochist, no matter how much inconvenience their stubborn insistence on saying "Yes" has caused. It is difficult to criticize the boss, because the boss has already attacked himself or herself more severely than you ever would. There is a natural tendency not to want to add to, but to assuage, anguish. But nothing you do or say soothes the boss, even though it seems obvious that comfort is what he or she yearning for.

I once read that a masochist in one setting is likely to be a masochist in another. That is what my boss was—a masochist. I read about them in a magazine in the reception area while I was waiting for my dentist appointment. Sandra was just like what I read in the magazine. She would come to work every morning exhausted. Her husband was starting a small business and when Sandra got off work here, she would go home and work all night to help him. She said he got angry if she was tired and didn't pitch in. All day long, she would drag her feet and act real gloomy. Well, his business was just about to open the week that we were asked about when we wanted to take our leave. I thought for sure she was going to ask off when the business opened, but she didn't. I asked her why not, but she had no explanation. She was entitled to the vacation, and she needed it. But she wouldn't take it. She just said she could handle everything and continued to drag around. *(payroll coordinator, female, age 43)*

Employees will probably feel guilty and eventually angry about being unable to console the boss. After a while, employees will begin to suffocate—to feel devitalized and fatigued by their futile rescue attempts. Feeling frustrated by the masochist's insatiable dependency needs, the employee has the propensity to grow resentful of the boss. But any accusations and hostility play into the masochist's hands. You may have feelings of shame and doubt that stem from your own incompetencies in making the boss feel better. But you also will likely feel that you can't escape—that you can't abandon the boss. In essence, then, the boss blackmails the employee with his or her suffering. You feel as if you are holding the masochist's lifeline, and if you let go, someone will surely come along and cut it.

WHEN THE MASOCHISTIC BOSS LOOKS IN THE MIRROR

If the employee ever hints that this forlorn presentation of the boss is disguised manipulation, the boss is likely to be shocked and distressed at being so terribly misunderstood. But in a way, manipulation is exactly what the boss is doing. As we all do, masochists have an underlying need to be loved and nurtured and they are willing to endure almost any form of humiliation, mistreatment, and pain to ensure they are accepted and cared for.

At the same time, masochists despise themselves for their dependency. They are ashamed of their willingness to accept abuse, but they fear being independent and assertive. They are afraid of succumbing to their belief that they are insignificant beings in a vast, uncaring world.

When employees withdraw their support, either through an attitude of indifference or through quitting, the boss feels rejected, resentful, and angry. But the masochist does not express hostility openly. Instead, the boss expresses fury through suffering and misery, by appearing exploited and injured. Masochists rarely express overt hostility, but they aggravate those who don't satisfy their needs by appearing, quite simply, pathetic. If the suffering ploy doesn't get the desired response, the masochist might try to win adoration through provocation. Of course, this doesn't work either. Thus, the masochist is bound to be frustrated and indignant.

Masochistic bosses freely admit their misery because they feel it is no disgrace to show their imperfections to the world. In fact, they believe their "openness" and their self-critical comments are evidence of their underlying honesty and humility. When masochistic bosses share their true despondency with another, they feel as if they are giving the gift of intimacy. They ardently desire to share their grief with another unhappy individual. Happy people are seen as superficial beings who are not in touch with the pain of this world. Therefore, the intimate other is invited to drop his or her cheery facade and release his or her pent-up pain. In this way, they can console each other and honestly share their grief—a masochistic grief-orgy, of sorts.

> Mark, the headwaiter, was always asking the rest of us why we didn't get tired of getting dumped on. He would always try to convince us that things were worse than they really were. And he would bring up everything—from taxes to lousy schedules to high interest rates. Honestly, I just wasn't that down about things. Maybe I am just out of touch, but it didn't seem so bad to me. But when he would get someone to go along with him, he was in heaven. They would wallow in pity for hours. Poor me, poor you became the theme of the shift. It was a real downer. Then, the owner would appear and ask someone to take a double shift and Mark would volunteer. I guess it gave him more ammunition for his pity party. *(waiter, male, age 21)*

Masochists see themselves as setting a moral example about how to behave and relate in this unfriendly world. From their perspective, we are all innocent victims and imperfect human beings who can unite in a holy communion by sharing our common misfortunes. We can then be honest, authentic human beings who are the ideals of dignity and morality, standing united in tragic suffering. At their core, masochistic bosses would like to be saintly. But if sainthood is not possible, then they will readily accept the role of martyr, as they believe inherent virtue is found in pain and suffering, self-criticism, and self-denial.

I think we all kind of felt sorry for Leticia. She was constantly covering for everyone else. Like one time, we were at a staff meeting. The head of another department was being bawled out for firing someone and the company was being sued for "wrongful termination" or something. Anyway, out of nowhere, Leticia spoke up and said she had encouraged the other department head to fire the worker. We were in shock. I don't think she even knew the guy who got axed. What was she thinking? Afterward, she explained that if the other department head got fired, he wouldn't be able to support his wife and three kids and she was single. Leticia was a real piece of work. *(meat processing supervisor, female, age 46)*

PRESCRIPTIONS FOR PERSEVERING

Don't Be the Masochist's Sadist

For your boss to be exploited, there must be an exploiter. Don't let this be you. If the masochistic boss sees you as someone who enjoys inflicting pain, you will become caught up in a sick, unending game of dominance and subservience. In essence, you will be perpetuating your boss's defect. So avoid faultfinding, criticizing, or taking advantage of your boss. No matter what the temptation to become tyrannical, resist it.

Don't Baby the Masochist by Spoon-Feeding Compliments

On the other hand, don't fall into the trap of constantly trying to console your dejected boss with spoon-fed compliments. If you do, your masochistic boss will be reinforced for playing the beaten-down, worn-out, and trampled-on victim. Remember, your well-intentioned efforts to pump up your boss will not be effective. The more you praise masochists, the more tempted they will be to proclaim their praiselessness.

Recognize the Masochist's Despair

If employees can tolerate and respect their bosses as human beings, the masochists will feel reassured, accepted, and loved. Be forewarned, however, that respect does not demand agreeing with all of the self-defacing comments the boss dishes out. If you go along with the boss's self-criticisms, you will be seen as uncaring. Instead, you need to empathize and be sensitive to the boss's pain. Show you are tuned in to the injustices of the world, but assure the boss that avoidance of these injustices can be a healthy response. Convince the boss that he or she does not have to willingly accept the burdens of the world alone in order to make it better.

Show Them There Doesn't Always Have to Be a Victim

Working for a masochistic puts you in the advantageous position of showing the boss that sometimes things can work out for the best—that sometimes things can go well for everyone. This will build the boss's confidence and cause him or her to question the need to always be the brunt of blame. Show the boss that if he or she would not try to undermine successes, there might be no blame. You can accomplish this by getting the boss involved in manageable, fail-proof projects for which they will be positively reinforced. The trick is to show the masochist there is more than one way to capture the attention and admiration of others. Show your boss that every scenario is not made up of aggressors and victims. Demonstrate to the masochist that some situations can be win-win for all involved.

10

The Dependent Boss:
The "I'm-Not-Okay,
but-Love-Me-Anyway" Type

No man is fit to command another that cannot command himself.

William Penn

DECIPHERING THE DEFECT

Dependent bosses can be thought of as organizational leeches. They latch onto someone else and depend upon that other individual for basic survival. Alone their future is uncertain. When joined to another, they feel secure. So they cling on for dear life, as a sky-diver would to a parachute, or a claustrophobic would to an open door. If you have ever had the feeling that someone else is shadowing you, and no matter how hard you try you cannot make the shadow disappear, then you have probably been a "benefactor." A benefactor is a tolerant individual in whom the dependent personality places unquestioned trust. Dependents rely upon and look to their benefactor for protection and shelter.

> I felt as if she was smothering me. It was as though someone had stuffed a pillow over my head and wouldn't let me breathe. Every day, she would ask where "we" were going to lunch. I wanted to tell her we were not handcuffed together, but I knew she wouldn't go eat by herself. And did she need to

eat! She must have weighed all of ninety pounds. When I took the job as her assistant, I didn't realize it would involve being her nutritionist, baby-sitter, bodyguard, and psychotherapist. But I could easily see why the tightwads down at City Hall were willing to let her have an assistant. She couldn't go to the bathroom by herself. *(administrative assistant to the librarian, female, age 31)*

Many dysfunctional bosses can't be recognized until they open their mouths, or until they stick their foot in them. But dependent bosses are different—they look different. Dependent bosses can usually be recognized by their stature. They tend to be either heavy and cumbersome (what medical types refer to as "endomorphic") or they tend to be thin and frail ("ectomorphic"). Some suggest, because of this unexplainable coincidence, that dependency is an unfortunate outgrowth of thyroid dysfunction. While such a rational medical explanation may induce employees to be more tolerant of their dependent defective boss, it certainly cannot be the whole answer.

Alvin reminded me of a possum—you know, he would roll over and play dead to protect himself. He would tell me, "I think we should do A." Then, when the director came in and said, "Let's do B," Alvin said "Great!" He was proud of the fact that he was compliant. In fact, he often "joked" that it was better to be a possum than an armadillo. For a long time, I never knew what that meant. Then I saw on one of those nature shows that when armadillos are threatened, like by a car traveling seventy miles and hour, they bristle and leap up. The car naturally hits them. Well, if I got nothing else out of that job, I learned two things—one about the animal kingdom and the other about how NOT to manage. *(snack machine vendor, male, age 34)*

Certainly, most dependent bosses have led sheltered lives. Few demands have been placed on them. They have likely been pampered and overprotected, and, as a result have not been forced to face the sometimes harsh realities of the "real" world. So they lack the competencies, skills, and coping mechanisms most normal people have. In short, they have never matured, and don't really want to start now. They see their purpose in life as ornamental, not functional.

Accordingly, dependent bosses are more than willing to abdicate total responsibility for their existence. This seems odd, particularly when a dependent personality has somehow reached the status of boss. In reality though, dependents are often granted supervisory positions because family members or close friends have a need to take care of or shelter the individual.

> I don't really know much about Whitney, except that she was raised with a silver spoon in her mouth. Oh, I also know that she is the niece of the owner. It seems her mother, the owner's sister, died when Whitney was about ten. I guess she took it pretty hard. So the owner sort of adopted her and gave her whatever she wanted, whenever she wanted it. And he still does. I think she got this job because he felt sorry for her. She certainly couldn't make it on her own. Whitney really isn't a bad boss. She is more like no boss at all. She is always down the hall with her uncle instead of being here. But I guess it could be worse. She really doesn't cause any harm and pretty much goes along with what we want as long as her uncle approves. *(cosmetic industry purchasing agent, male, age 46)*

The passive-dependent boss tends to be highly submissive. He or she has an entrenched and pervasive need for affection and approval. To get these needs met, dependents are quite willing to be nonassertive and to live according to the whims and dictates of others. In some cases, dependent personalities will find a benefactor among their subordinate ranks. But often, individuals lower in rank cannot ensure continued security. So the dependent turns his or her love-seeking groveling to higher-ups.

If the dependent boss can identify a willing benefactor among the higher ranks, he or she mighty be capable of functioning quite well. As long as the benefactor remains trustworthy and nurturing, the dependent boss can function with ease. And when at ease, dependents are typically giving and considerate of their employees.

So, dependents may not be altogether undesirable. In fact, they can be selfless, generous, and thoughtful. They readily accept blame for problems and are unduly apologetic. They are obsequious, humble, genteel, and even servile. They are accepting and warm, and don't even react to being the brunt of cruel office jokes. They have a Pollyanna-like attitude. Dependents trust and they are very loyal, in the anticipation that they will be cared for, supported, and nurtured. The only inkling of animosity that may ever arise is when the dependent becomes jealous that someone else is seeking the attention of his or her benefactor.

Dependents are self-effacing and have low self-esteem. Their lack of self-confidence shows in their mannerisms, posture, and speech. They tend to downplay their abilities, strengths, and achievements. In fact, dependents rigorously avoid expressing their opinions or suggestions. Instead, they kowtow to the desires of others. They feel unable to function independently or to assume responsibility. They leave major decisions to others and are quite willing to assist, but they do not want to be in the driver's seat, and never want to go out on a limb. Dependents never demand anything in return for their undying support, affirmation, and assistance. To expect others to reciprocate would risk abandonment.

> You know, I would be quite willing to forgo my Christmas bonus if my boss would just be willing to grow a backbone. He is not stupid, but to hear him tell it, he never had a good idea in his life. He is like a jellyfish, going only where the tide takes him. I have the feeling that if left to his own defenses, the world would just open its mouth and gobble him up. Really, it is a sad way to have to go through life. I wonder how he can respect himself. *(eyeglass lens optician, female, age 28)*

Diagnosing the Defect: Is Your Boss Dependent?

YES	NO		
_____	_____	1.	Do you often feel burdened by your boss's emotional needs?
_____	_____	2.	Would your boss rather you make decisions than make them himself or herself?

YES	NO		
_____	_____	3.	Does your boss act so helpless that you sometimes would like to kick him or her in the rear?
_____	_____	4.	Does your boss like to be taken care of?
_____	_____	5.	Is your boss so powerless that he or she seems to lack a backbone?
_____	_____	6.	Is it difficult for your boss to take the initiative or lead a group project?
_____	_____	7.	Under your boss's inadequacies, do you sense there is a melancholy person?
_____	_____	8.	Would your boss be willing to put himself or herself down in order to elicit support?
_____	_____	9.	Does your boss seem deficient in accomplishing tasks by himself or herself?
_____	_____	10.	Is the boss so clingy that you often get irritated?

If you answered "YES" to more than 7 questions, your boss exhibits strong dependent tendencies.

If you answered "YES" to between 4 and 7 questions, your boss exhibits moderate dependent tendencies.

PREDICTABLE REACTIONS TO THE PATHOLOGY

If your boss is dependent, and someone higher up is the boss's benefactor, you might as well forget the possibility of any direct supervision. Any of the normal things bosses do will be done only with the expressed approval and consent of the boss's benefactor. Employees who forget to remember that the boss is not capable of serving as a boss are doomed to frustration.

On the other hand, if you are cursed with the heavy obligation of being your boss's benefactor, you might as well forget the luxury of having an occasional bad day. Dependent bosses do not and cannot look inward for affirmation or reassurance. It all comes from someone else. If you are that someone, the boss depends on you for consistent, predictable nurturance. Dependents place their lives in your hands, which is often an unwelcome burden. Because of this, they will be very sensitive to your mood changes. They fear rejection and will relentlessly try to comply with their benefactor's wishes. They become submissive and acquiescent so that the nourishment from others continues to flow. But if it looks as if they are going to be cut off, dependents become anxious and apprehensive.

> Others warned me about my boss Jamie. But they weren't the usual warnings. Typically, the big bad boss is a tyrant, an ogre, the type that would go out of the way to kick an anthill. But not Jamie. Jamie was a different sort of bad boss. He would ask others, "Do you want me to kick over the anthill?" If they said "yes," he would. If they said "no," he wouldn't. He reminded me of my baby, which is probably why he didn't aggravate me as much as he did the others. Jamie and my baby were both experiencing "separation anxiety." The baby would whimper when I left for work and Jamie would whimper when I left for home. But I wasn't sure Jamie would grow out of it. *(floral arranger, female, age 32)*

The dependent's constant need for attention and assurance may quickly become aggravating. However, abandonment of the dependent boss only makes him or her more needy. Benefactors, contemplating the none-too-soon rejection of their dependent boss, will find him or her to be even more ingratiating, more clinging, and more desperate. Irritation intensifies, as does more pleading and promising by the boss. This ploy serves him or her quite well. The dependent's meek, docile, desperate behavior compels benefactors to stay on board. After all, how can you sacrifice this helpless, self-sacrificing urchin of a boss?

WHEN THE DEPENDENT BOSS
LOOKS IN THE MIRROR

Dependents are like actors facing a hostile audience. They must play a role that is pleasing to the audience, even if that role is totally inconsistent with their innermost feelings. On the surface, they must be optimistic. Dependents always seem to see the silver lining in the situation, no matter how low the dark cloud is looming. They seem to put on rose-colored glasses to block out the bad in the world and its people. They constrict their view of the ugly. After all, to openly express contempt, fear, or displeasure would be a downer. Who wants to be around a party pooper?

But not too far below the surface of this warm, optimistic being lies a serious and melancholy individual struggling to keep up a sanguine image. That is paramount. To reveal their true persona, to share their fears, to expose their doubts, would be to risk abandonment. So they frantically pursue acceptance and approval from others. In reality, life brings dependents little joy. But their dismay is adamantly suppressed. They would rather suffer in silence than suffer alone.

Psychotherapists refer to the dependent's clinginess as "introjection"—the tendency to develop an intense devotion to another. Introjection goes beyond just identification or casual attachment. It involves the whole internalization of another with the hope of creating an impenetrable and unbreakable bond. Dependents lose their own identity and become subsumed into their benefactor. They willingly sacrifice their independence and autonomy, hoping to prevent conflict and strengthen the relationship with those they are dependent upon.

So dependents assume the role of the loyal servant, or the loyal court jester. They present themselves as noncompetitive and modest in their ambitions, but beneath their exterior, they feel inadequate and insecure. They exaggerate their deficits and flaws and downgrade their merits. They emphasize their inabilities and handicaps, sometimes to the point of fantasizing leg, arm, or back problems. This way, they can cast themselves off as disabled.

By putting themselves down, dependents try to evoke support and empathy. In effect, their self-deprecation can be viewed as a ploy for ensuring sustenance from others. It also serves the useful purpose of precluding them from having to take on too many responsibilities.

What is particularly interesting about the dependent is that they spew out so much self-deprecating rhetoric, that they begin to believe it themselves. Dependents somehow convince themselves that they cannot do any better. They trick themselves into accepting their dependency as the one and only way. They see themselves as inferior and inadequate, and they come to believe that they will never be able to function as an independent, self-sustaining individual. The power of suggestion is indeed a powerful tool.

> I guess if you tell yourself something for long enough, you come to believe it. I think that is what happened to Toby. He was always saying how the most important thing was loyalty to the company. He was particularly attached to the vice president. We made tennis racquets. We were small and we had to be lean to compete with the big manufacturers. Toby really didn't add much. So finally, the president fired him. When Toby found out all he worried about was how the vice president would be disappointed in him. He was still loyal, even after they axed him. *(product tester, male, age 25)*

PRESCRIPTIONS FOR PERSEVERING

Don't Take the Bait

Though dependent bosses claim to be incompetent, the motivation for this chastisement derives from their desire to be supported and nurtured. Unfortunately, this self-deprecation often serves to convince others of their limited capabilities. When this happens, employees fall into the trap, they take the bait. Fostering the boss's dependence simply guarantees others of the perpetual role of caretaker. Instead of buying into the boss's ploy of helplessness, give him or her some hope. Help dependents build their self-esteem by showing them that they can, they should, they must exercise some independent discretion. But don't become domineering, lest you become a benefactor. Instead, encourage growth through a humanistic approach. Don't simply demand it or expect that it will happen over-night. The maturation process takes time.

Don't Accept Subservience; Insist on Supervision

Dependent bosses fear failure. So to avoid potential embarrass-ment, they refrain from acquiring the skills they need to succeed. To accommodate for their technical inadequacy, they try to be good-natured, charitable, and accommodating. But such stuff does not make good managers. For a while, employees may cherish the laissez-faire style of the dependent boss. But at some point, you may actually need someone to fill the role of boss. In all likelihood, the dependent will not be ready for that challenge. That is, unless, you foster "bossish" behavior. Ask the boss for assistance even when you don't need it. Let the boss make decisions of little conse-quence and implement them. Then progress from there. The idea is to get the boss to take baby steps. If you don't, he or she might never be up to speed, creating a leadership vacuum in your work world.

If They Can't Lead, Let Them Follow

Dependent bosses are more skilled at following than at leading. They are more skilled at assisting than at commanding. And they like, they prefer, to play the "second." In that capacity, they can assist, take blame for failures, and generally make themselves indis-pensable to others. So, they avoid expressions of power. If the dependent boss abdicates authority, there are some cases where it may be okay just to go ahead and accept it. Take the bull by the horns instead of using valuable time trying to get the boss to take charge. After all, someone has to get the job done. Just keep the boss informed, and let him or her participate to whatever extent the two of you feel is realistic.

Don't Go AWOL

As long as the vast needs of dependents are being satisfied, they feel safe in their world. Their worst fear is abandonment. Isolation creates a void in them that only others can fill. On their own, dependents are unable to make even simple decisions without another to rely on. They become immobilized and destitute. They feel lost, fragile, weak, and helpless when alone. Recognize this and learn to tolerate it. It will feel like you are attached at the hip, but don't try to sever the bond all at once. To do so would be to encourage greater dependence. And in the end, independence is the utopian outcome.

11

The Depressive Boss:
The "I-Can't-Pull-My-Head-
Up-Off-My-Chin" Type

When we cannot find contentment in ourselves, it is useless to seek it elsewhere.

La Rochefoucauld

DECIPHERING THE DEFECT

Although much has been written lately about "workplace depression," it is not a disease of deindustrialization or downsizing. On the contrary, social history tells us that leaders and laborers, intellectuals and idiots, and the prosperous and poor alike have suffered from depression since the beginning of time. In Ancient Greece, melancholia was believed to be the result of "imbalanced humors" in the body, specifically an excess of black bile. In the Middle Ages, depressives were imprisoned and tortured. And, as late as the nineteenth century, leeches were applied to the bodies of depressives to suck out the evil and free their sad spirits.

Given the pervasiveness of depressives today, we can conclude none of these cures proved successful. In fact, we are now seeing spin-offs of the basic depressive constellation. "Layoff Survivor's Syndrome" is one such diagnosis. It is a "condition" that results when workers live through massive terminations, but somehow retain their positions. Despair, dejection, and despondency result because these "fortunate" individuals are left to wait for the next ax to fall. Indeed, the environment is right for depression.

There are two "garden varieties" of depression. The first is labeled "reactive." Reactive depression is a mood disorder that can be directly traced to an event, such as the death of a loved one, divorce or desertion, demotion or discharge. It can last up to several months, as a normal part of the "grief" process. The grief process entails five stages: (1) denial ("this is not happening to me"); (2) anger ("it is your fault this is happening to me"); (3) bargaining ("if you can stop this from happening, I will make it worth your while"); (4) depression ("things will never be the same again"); and (5) acceptance ("things will never be the same, but that is OK"). On a positive note, depressives eventually move from the depression to the acceptance stage.

The second type of depression is less transitory. It is labeled "endogenous" depression, and it arises for no apparent reason and without a real trigger. Some have suggested causes might include genetic tendencies, sunlight deprivation, social isolation, stress, and biochemical flaws (e.g., an imbalance of trace metals such as copper and lithium). But since the true cause of endogenous depression is unknown, preventing it is impossible.

With both types of depression, there are common symptoms and reactions. In the eyes of her staff members, Sandy, a regional manager for a major airline, experienced all of them. They are listed below.

- An alteration of moods, in which the individual becomes increasingly more hopeless, sad, lonely, and apathetic.

  I do not know what happened to Sandy, but over time you could see her slumping into oblivion. It was like she was caught in a drain, and she kept sinking further and further. It had been hard for her. She was young and relatively new on the job. But she was hired just as others were being pushed out the door. Almost from the day Sandy arrived, she had to start handing out pink slips to single mothers, to men who had been on the job for thirty-seven years, to people who had trusted her. It became very macabre. I almost wanted to encourage her to quit. But she seemed so unresponsive, so distant. *(reservation agent, female, age 31)*

- Negative self-concept and blame.

  I think somewhere, deep inside her, Sandy felt responsible for the layoffs. It made no sense, because everyone knew she had absolutely nothing to do with it. She was just the messenger, sort of the "black angel." But by blaming herself, she lost her focus. She could have been of more help to all of us. Sandy could have restructured, investigated transfers, and encouraged outplacement. But she did none of this. *(baggage handler, male, age 37)*

- Regressive and self-punitive wishes; the individual feels as if the future is futile and death is inviting.

    It wasn't a very funny time, but every now and then we would try to lighten the mood, even if it was with black humor. For example, I remember one time we joked with Sandy about one of the "terminals" (as we called them) returning to the airport and shooting things up. You know, like you see in the paper. OK, so it wasn't that funny, but you know what Sandy said? She remarked that she would deserve such a fate. And the scary part was, I think she meant it. *(flight attendant, female, age 34)*

- Desire to escape or hide, to detach oneself, and be in isolation.

    I know she was going through a bad time, but so were we. We looked to her for guidance, for reassurance, for leadership. I hate to be crass, but her sulkiness didn't do anything to help the subterranean morale around the place. She didn't come out, she didn't mingle, she stayed cooped up in the back. I would sometimes ask her to help me deal with a passenger just to get her circulating. *(gate agent, female, age 42)*

- Eating disorders and weight loss.
- An inability to fall asleep or an inability to wake up.

    Sandy began to look like a walking corpse. I guess I never realized a person's mood could take such a physical toll. She wasn't eating, and it looked like she wasn't sleeping. Finally we stopped looking to her for support. She could barely support herself. In the end, I think she quit. I really hope she ended up in a more tranquil environment. *(reservation agent, male, age 24)*

Depressive bosses take little pleasure in work or leisure activities. In fact, they take little pleasure in anything. Depressives generally experience pervasive negativity, that is, they are not only dissatisfied with their own state but are also displeased with the world in general. They seem to react critically in most situations, feeling anguish, anger, contempt, disgust, guilt, fear, shame, and sadness.

But while sadness may be the emotion most often associated with depression, employees working for a depressive may also notice their boss's tendencies toward being irritable, upset, and nervous. Depressives typically look more stressed and strained than they should in any given situation. They also seem pessimistic about what the future holds. Depressives expect the worst, have a hard time relaxing, and rarely believe things will go their way.

Statistics tell us the profile most susceptible to depression is a middle-aged woman. Females may be more likely to be depressed than men because of the number of role conflicts women have in our society compared to men (wife, mother, management of the home, and worker). And, in the workplace, women are likely to be thwarted by the glass ceiling and are typically underpaid. Another reason is that women are more likely to blame themselves for their personal and organizational failures. Men, on the other hand, have been found more likely to project blame onto others. This enables males to bolster their self-esteem and avoid some of the negative emotions associated with depression.

Diagnosing the Defect: Is Your Boss Depressive?

YES   NO

_____   _____   1. Does your boss seem helpless and inadequate, almost at the mercy of events?

_____   _____   2. Does your boss demonstrate very flat affect and/or does he or she fail to exhibit any positive emotions?

_____   _____   3. Is your boss hopeless about the workplace in particular, but also about the world in general?

_____   _____   4. Is your boss usually pessimistic and negative?

YES   NO

_____   _____   5.   Does your boss seem to be "alone" and melancholy even in a crowd?

_____   _____   6.   Is your boss self-deprecating?

_____   _____   7.   Does it seem as though your boss is impotent rather than omnipotent?

_____   _____   8.   Does your boss seem unable to experience anything pleasurable, such as laughing or joking?

_____   _____   9.   Has your boss lost interest in and motivation to work?

_____   _____   10.   Is it difficult for your boss to concentrate on or take an interest in anything that is work-related?

If you answered "YES" to more than 7 questions, your boss exhibits strong depressive tendencies.

If you answered "YES" to between 4 and 7 questions, your boss exhibits moderate depressive tendencies.

PREDICTABLE REACTIONS TO THE PATHOLOGY

Initially, the depressive boss's guilt, shame, and feelings of blameworthiness may cause us to be sympathetic. Depressives feel that they have suffered from more stressful events than the rest of us, and indeed many have. This stimulates us to be tolerant and possibly assume the role of cheerleader.

But like influenza, depression is contagious. Depressive bosses create a downtrodden environment and dampen employee spirit. Their emotionless facade becomes the dress of the day.

> I have heard that, on average, people laugh fifteen times a day and that laughter can be very healing. We tried to joke with him, but Jake's sense of humor was zilch. Then, just to get a rise out of him, we unconsciously started trying to anger him.

All we wanted was a response, any response. Eventually, we all stopped trying. *(automotive worker, male, age 28)*

You instinctively want to reassure your boss that things will be okay, that it will get better. But such reassurances are met by deaf ears. Or, if heard, the depressive boss will likely question your sincerity and sanity. At some point, the employee will give up this futile charade.

Trying to make the boss "feel better" will not carry any weight with depressives. Again, their condemnation spills over from just blaming themselves to blaming the employees in the unit. Depressive bosses are likely to overestimate the size of mistakes. Any ambiguous information they pick up is interpreted negatively. And, they are inclined to attribute problems to employee incompetence rather than to the adversity of the situation.

"It is the employee's fault" is the depressive bosses' immediate reaction. They believe workers usually are blameworthy. And, in extreme cases, depressive bosses will insist that staff members intentionally acted to cause them distress.

Because of the boss's negativity and propensity to cast a wide net of blame, employees become increasingly detached from the depressive boss. Employees learn to dislike, and therefore, avoid depressives. As a result, the depressive boss finds he or she has fewer and fewer people to talk to at work, further exacerbating the feeling of isolation.

WHEN THE DEPRESSIVE BOSS LOOKS IN THE MIRROR

Depressives suffer from such excessive guilt that it could probably be better characterized as "shame." All of us have, at some time, felt guilty about doing something we probably should not have. This is normal. But when an individual experiences shame, he or she is concerned not just about one behavior but with one's total self-concept. Depressives are ashamed of themselves, of their entire being. To combat this, they will attempt to externalize blame. Depressives will freely share blame with and castigate others for their own problems, totally unaware of how their projection of blame affects others.

Associated with this painful shame is the feeling of being small, worthless, and powerless. Depressives anticipate public disapproval. While alone, they imagine how they must appear to other people, and they want to hide and disappear. Therefore, depressives usually have an inactive social life. While some depressives project an aura of sociability and seem to have many outside contacts, the quality of the interactions often leaves them feeling lonely. In the depressive's relationships, there is less intimacy, enjoyment, and responsiveness.

At home, depressives have trouble relaxing. They have a decreased sexual drive, suffer from constipation, and are easily fatigued. They feel confused, hopeless, and empty. They have doubts about their adequacy and have feelings of worthlessness, leading to occasional thoughts about suicide.

They obsess about negative feedback and seem unable or unwilling to process positive feedback. They freely spew out self-deprecating statements, increasing their dissatisfaction with life. Rather than coping with adaptive emotional strategies such as acceptance, humor, or positive reframing of a crisis, depressives tend to be stuck using denial. Instead of trying to fix the problem, they repress its existence or blame others for it. They do not actively try to solve their problems.

As a result, most of us are more tolerant of depressives if they handle their ordeal alone and do not involve us in their difficulties. Although we might wish they weren't so melancholy, if depressives have to suffer, we prefer they suffer in silence.

PRESCRIPTIONS FOR PERSEVERING

Let Depression Take Its Natural Course

Much advice has been offered on how to cure depressives. Recommendations range from stress management, to herbal tea, to drops of sage oil in their bathwater. But the reality seems to be that there is no cure-all. Depressives don't want to be depressed, although they generally lack the motivation to help themselves. They are victimized by a pattern of desolation, despondency, and hopelessness.

Aspirations of getting better do not seem to be present. But, as aggravating as depressives are, they cannot shake themselves out of their funk, nor can you do it for them. In fact, research shows that those who are chronically depressed are likely to remain this way throughout their careers even when they change jobs and occupations. Genetic makeup has been identified as an influence in the depressive's negative view of life.

Do not encourage the depressive to "cheer up," or to "get a good night's sleep." Instead, say something such as, "With all the terrible things that have happened to you, I am surprised you are holding up so well. I would be in much worse shape." That way, when the depressive compares himself or herself to you, things might not seem so bad.

Don't Take It Personally

Depressive bosses are quick to blame others for difficulties in the workplace. But instead of growing defensive, try not to personalize their projections and accusations. Instead, try to see their insinuations as their way of dealing with their shame.

Count to Ten and Jump Back In

Employees have different degrees of tolerance and empathy for the depressive boss. A select few individuals may be extremely patient, but most employees become aggravated by the boss's repeated demands for reassurance. At some point, employees become exasperated and give up trying to provide assistance. Instead, they reject the boss. However, this only increases the boss's depression. Instead of perpetuating the depressive's isolation, try to include him of her in the goings-on of the workplace.

Show Them Who Is in Control

Depressive bosses lack initiative and have feelings of being powerless. They are in a state of learned helplessness. They have lost control, feeling that both success and failure are outside of their range of influence. Depressive bosses seem to lack access and awareness of the actions to take to make their life better. They not only lack emotional stamina, they also have an inordinate inability to concentrate or make decisions. Lucidity is a luxury not all of us have. Through demonstrating confidence in and showing support for the depressive boss, you might be able to instill some feelings of empowerment.

12

The Anxious Boss:
The "I'm-So-Scared,
Please-Don't-Hurt-Me" Type

It is a miserable thing to live in suspense; it is the life of a spider.

Jonathan Swift

DECIPHERING THE DEFECT

Anxious bosses are organizational hermits. But they don't just slink into seclusion, they actively bury themselves there. Generally uncomfortable in the presence of others, anxious bosses find themselves in quite a predicament, since by definition supervision involves other individuals. Working for an anxious boss presents a challenge similar to the one depicted in the film *Catch-22*, in which the boss invites workers to his office only when he is not there!

Anxious bosses must be distinguished from those who are, quite simply, unsociable. Unsociable bosses don't like people, which is why they avoid interaction. In contrast, anxious bosses avoid contact with others because they are fearful, because they are scared. Those suffering from anxiety are introverted, aloof, and seclusive. They never "let their hair down" and they are isolated and lonely by their own choice and because of their own doings. But it would be incorrect to assume that anxious bosses revel in their isolation. In fact, just the opposite is true.

Anxious bosses would love to be part of the gang; they would kill to be in the in-crowd. They long to be invited on hunting trips or shopping trips, or even to lunch. But they won't, they can't, take the first step toward interacting with their co-workers. Their fear of rejection and humiliation is just too powerful. Their self-esteem is too incredibly low. While anxious bosses would like to be more outgoing, their fear of being shunned, brushed off, or disapproved of dominates. It is a conflictual world in which they fluctuate between a desire for affection and a fear of rejection, all the while regretting their isolated existence. But, in the end, anxious bosses are just too worrisome to do anything about their social desires.

> Bruce ate alone in the cafeteria, usually with a book jammed up against his spectacles. I don't think he was really reading. He just wanted to ward off any potential conversation. Every now and then, when a burst of laughter would float through the cafeteria, he would look up. But if anyone made any advances toward him, he would go back to the book. I always felt like Bruce was lonely. But he never seemed to want to join in. So we left him alone. *(investment counselor, female, age 31)*

Unfortunately, anxious bosses' attempts at self-preservation and protection only serve to compound their problems in the work environment. Anxious bosses refuse to join in; they take breaks by themselves, they avoid holiday gatherings, birthday celebrations, and company picnics, creating an aura of "being above it all." Furthermore, anxious bosses warily scan for threats that aren't present; they overreact to innocuous events, and they anticipate being mocked. Paradoxically, these abnormal behaviors often promote ridicule—the thing they most dread.

Most anxious bosses would rather not be in management. The reason they often end up there is because they were proficient at doing the jobs for which they were trained, usually in highly technical areas. A typically forgotten fact is that anxious people select technical careers because they want jobs in which they don't have to interact too much; most work is done individually or with other people like them. The Peter Principle is operative here—anxious bosses truly are promoted to their level of incompetence. Usually this happens to anxious bosses under silent protest.

> Cliff was socially inept. He always kept a safe distance, and was never comfortable when others were around. I once

asked—I just had to—how he got to be a department head. He quickly, but quietly answered, "Because I am the least qualified." I thought his response was sort of funny, but there was no sign of amusement in his face. I think supervision was like torture to Cliff. Between disciplinary actions and employee recognition ceremonies, Cliff tried to get some projects out. He wasn't expected to, but that is what he enjoyed doing. I think that helped him to keep his sanity. *(city planner, male, age 36)*

Such promotions to management do, indeed, take a physical toll. Anxious bosses are highly prone to panic attacks. While it is true that nearly one-third of the population has experienced a panic attack at some point in their lives, most do not suffer through them continuously. The anxious boss does. The signs of a panic attack are telltale—difficulty breathing, heart pounding, dry mouth, chest pains, tingling hands and feet, sweating, trembling, and a foreboding sense of fear. Some anxious people actually panic to the point of paralysis.

When such symptoms manifest it is difficult for anxious bosses to hold a coherent conversation. Their anxiety distracts them and interferes with their ability to concentrate. Yet don't attribute the anxious boss's jittery and disjointed behavior to a failure to pay attention. Just the opposite is true. In social situations, anxious bosses operate on high alert. All the while you are interacting with them, they are closely monitoring your moods and feelings.

Before the boss will even slightly open up to you, he or she will want an unconditional guarantee that you will offer total and uncritical acceptance. He or she will become distant at the first hint of rejection. Although all of us are concerned with how others see us, the anxious boss is crushed by even slight hints of spurning.

It is hard to label a likeable guy like Ron as a bad manager, but in my opinion, he is. The most important thing in the world to him is that everyone likes him. As a result, people that work for Ron take advantage of him. I am not sure whether he realizes that or not. I clearly remember my first day—I was shocked. Everyone was acting so unprofessional and disrespectful. Ron seemed to be the brunt of distasteful jokes and the others did not try too hard to conceal their mockery. He provided no structure at all, which left most of us "spinning our wheels" half the time. When Ron would call meetings, people wouldn't bother to show up and they didn't even bother to offer excuses. Instead of Ron running the office, the office was running Ron. *(mortgage banker, female, age 29)*

It is physically and emotionally exhausting to the anxious boss just to make it through the day. Five minutes of intense exchanges with others can seem more tiring than a long day of hard, physical labor. By the time they leave work, anxious people often have poor appetites and they feel drained and fatigued. Yet they cannot relax. They become so "worked up" from dealing with others at work that it takes them a long time to "come down" and relax. They deliberate at length about the accumulated unpleasantness of the day. As a result, many anxious bosses suffer from insomnia. It is a taxing lifestyle, and anxious bosses know it. People suffering from anxiety recognize that they have a problem, and this serves to magnify their misery.

Diagnosing the Defect: Is Your Boss Anxious?

YES   NO

_____ _____ 1. Does your boss typically seem nervous even in casual get-togethers?

_____ _____ 2. Is it impossible for your boss to relax while in the presence of strangers?

_____ _____ 3. Does your boss hesitate to call or contact people he or she does not know?

_____ _____ 4. Does your boss avoid chances to get to know new people?

_____ _____ 5. Is your boss painfully uncomfortable when he or she meets someone for the first time?

YES	NO	
_____	_____	6. Does being introduced to new people make your boss apprehensive?
_____	_____	7. Does your boss seem vulnerable and easily embarrassed?
_____	_____	8. Does your boss create excuses to avoid going to social events?
_____	_____	9. Does your boss suffer from frequent panic attacks?
_____	_____	10. Is it difficult for your boss to maintain his or her train of thought during conversations because of nervousness?

If you answered "YES" to more than 7 questions, your boss exhibits strong anxiety tendencies.

If you answered "YES" to between 4 and 7 questions, your boss exhibits moderate anxiety tendencies.

PREDICTABLE REACTIONS TO THE PATHOLOGY

Anxious bosses are, by definition, "avoidant," which means they tend to shy away from social interaction and they get nervous when they are forced to converse. To the casual observer, the anxious boss may appear apprehensive, vulnerable, on edge, uptight, and fretful. And the anxious boss is. Anxious-avoidants are awkward and constricted in social exchanges. Because of their uncomfortableness, the employee is likely to feel that conversations are strained and stilted.

Anxious bosses typically speak slowly, deliberately, and hesitantly. They pause, stumble over sentence fragments, appear confused, and often digress. Their body language is stiff and constrained. What movements they do make are often fidgety or nervous twitches and are often precursors to panic attacks. As soon as the anxious boss detects the opportunity, he or she will attempt to escape your company. This leaves some employees feeling as if their efforts to talk to the boss are unwelcome intrusions.

On the surface, anxious bosses truly do seem unresponsive. They will minimize affect or emotion and give the appearance of being cold and withdrawn. But those employees who know them well are aware that underneath they are timid and sensitive, kind and accommodating. Unfortunately, very few ever get to know the anxious boss that well.

> Stanley has been the local manager at my financial services company for four years. Before he got promoted, he was a research analyst. Stanley graduated from a prestigious all-male college here in the city, and that really helps to attract clients. The funny thing is, the clients often don't remember him from school, although he seems to remember them. Anyway, there was an older gentleman in the department who was constantly patting and putting his arm around the receptionist. The receptionist had repeatedly spoken to Stanley about the harassment, but he never did anything about it. I know he wanted to help but he just couldn't take action. In fact, I think he hated to see her come into his office because he knew she was coming to complain. The receptionist finally quit and sued the company. She won, but the whole problem could have been prevented if Stanley would have been firm. *(personal credit advisor, female, age 29)*

Their tense and fearful presentation prevents anxious bosses from performing important and essential managerial duties. For example, they detest networking, so they won't engage in the political maneuvering it often takes to advance the careers of their employees (or themselves). As a result, their debilitating anxiety interferes with an employee's climb up the organizational ladder. Even worse, anxious bosses will sometimes totally avoid newcomers to the unit, which doesn't do much for the boss's respect or confidence factors. Antics such as these may cause employees to be critical and to scorn the ineffectiveness of the boss, which makes him or her even more avoidant.

Another common complaint derives from the boss's unwillingness to defend and protect employees. Anxious bosses are particularly useless in conflicts of any sort. In fact, they are usually too busy trying to minimize the problem and reframe the issue in a positive light instead of facing the ugly realities of the situation.

> The problem with Danny is that he just doesn't act like a boss. He is very sympathetic and accommodating, but he refuses to take control when problems arise. He doesn't want to be in charge. Danny calls it delegating, but I call it abdicating. He always wants those of us who work for him to "patch things up" on our own. Every morning before he comes in, Danny calls to see if there are any problems. It is like he is testing the water. If trouble is brewing, he just won't make an appearance. *(air traffic controller, male, age 42)*

Particularly threatening is the performance appraisal interview, in which the anxious boss must judge another. This event certainly doesn't allow for the uncritical acceptance that he or she so desperately seeks. Yet anxious bosses recognize that if they only appease the most incompetent employees, they will lose what little personal integrity they have been able to salvage.

Anxious bosses are insecure in disputes and noncommittal on issues. They are capable of making only piecemeal changes because they can't decide on what direction to follow. So first they decide on a direction to please someone (a boss or employee), then they switch directions to please another. This erratic behavior and confused demeanor is infuriating. Yet any sign of aggravation will cause anxious bosses to lose track of their stream of thought. The overwhelming stress prevents them from being good problem-solvers. They do not perform well under pressure, and they generally avoid the risks associated with creative thoughts. Group exercises such as brainstorming are a terrible challenge.

WHEN THE ANXIOUS BOSS
LOOKS IN THE MIRROR

A continuous battle rages inside the psyche of anxious bosses—one part of them wants to be gregarious, but the other part of them is paralyzed with fear over being rebuffed or humiliated. Since their fear wins, they consciously avoid contact with others. Distance is preferred to dialogue. Solitude is preferred to socializing. Retreat is preferred to rejection.

> The problem with Marla was that no one respected her and she didn't bother to earn or even demand respect. She managed sales-people, who were typically outgoing and friendly. Maria was just the opposite. She avoided the staff like the plague. It didn't take long for us to recognize that. She didn't care where we were just as long as we were not bothering her. This care-free (or care-less) attitude of hers encouraged us to go skiing or to play golf when we were supposed to be in the office or with clients. But we didn't worry because we knew she would never do anything to us. *(sales rep, male, age 28)*

When they are forced from their reclusiveness, anxious bosses absorb a great deal of stimuli. This abundance of stimuli is some-times overwhelming to these sensitive beings, and it distracts them from the main and relevant points of the interaction. They worry about how they come across to others, how they are going to get through a social discourse, if they will do something socially awk-ward, and if someone will say something painful or embarrassing. These distractions and internal turmoil interfere with the anxious boss's thinking abilities. Therefore, his or her diminished cognitive function-ing makes the boss appear less capable and competent than he or she really is.

Anxious bosses engage in chronic introspection and self-inves-tigation, which prevents them from hiding from their feelings of inadequacy. They experience ongoing psychic conflict and inner tension. And, they ruminate excessively about humiliations (both real and imagined) suffered at the hands of others. With little tangi-ble evidence, the anxious boss feels as if others slight, snub, dislike, and even despise him or her. Thus they remain ill at ease and highly self-conscious.

But their defense of turning away from others brings them little comfort. They are ashamed of their social fears and despise them-selves for their anxieties. Then they become contemptuous of them-selves, blaming themselves for being inadequate and bringing on some of the rejection shoveled their way. They engage in self-contempt because they can't accept their shortcomings and are sure that others can't either. They believe it is futile to try to improve their life. They are perfectionistic, having excessively high personal standards, and they overmonitor their own performance. The messages they give themselves are: they must perform well, must win the approval of the group, and must not experience discomfort, even though they expect that doom is approaching.

If you ever get the chance to know the anxious boss better, his or her unfounded concerns about unrealistic catastrophes will become evident. His of her life revolves around avoiding threatening situations, which is a full-time preoccupation since the anxious boss will read threat into nearly all situations and even interpret benign information as threatening. Anxious bosses will focus on the worst. For example, a statement such as "His convictions were not widely known" may create fantasies of court proceedings and jail terms. They dwell on the word "convictions," which elicits grave concerns, when the term was used to refer to "beliefs" rather than to imagined incarceration.

Since anxious bosses seldom venture outside their own protected world, they tend to create rich fantasies to satisfy their social yearnings. They daydream, write in diaries, and watch TV, providing themselves with a safe forum for expressing feelings and emotions too dangerous to express to others.

PRESCRIPTIONS FOR PERSEVERING

You Can't Judge This Book by Its Cover

The slow, sluggish behavior sometimes exhibited by the anxious boss is deceptive, because under the surface is a hyperalert and vigilant being who is exquisitely sensitive to the environment. Anxious bosses take in much more than you realize. They are very cognizant of the feelings and intentions of others. For this reason you should carefully monitor your own nonverbals, avoiding any signs of exasperation, contempt, or ill will.

Say It with a Memo

Because of their constant and sensitive scanning of the workplace, anxious bosses are likely to pick up on the interpersonal conflicts and problems they wish to avoid. Only distance allows them the safety they need to avoid such potentially threatening situations. So respect their need for seclusion. When possible, leave phone messages or use electronic mail to correspond. These impersonal forms of communication will be preferred by your anxious boss.

The anxious boss is an introverted rather than an extroverted being. The extrovert requires stimulation from the environment to become aroused; the introvert has a high level of internal arousal. When the introvert wakes up in the morning, his or her level of arousal is already so high that outside stimulation pushes it beyond an optimum level. To alleviate the stress associated with too much arousal, the introvert avoids the stimulation associated with interacting with people.

Additionally, introverted bosses don't like to be interrupted. Instead, they prefer to work alone, dealing with ideas and working on tasks requiring careful attention. They are not as talkative nor can they express their ideas as clearly as those who are more extroverted. So don't march into your boss's office unannounced, expecting or demanding instant satisfaction.

Be the Boss's Mouthpiece

To balance the introverted boss's style, employees can volunteer whenever possible to do the things that the boss hates, such as dealing with others. This is particularly necessary in the afternoon when the introvert gets worn down, but the extrovert is just warming up. Let the boss attend to less stimulating tasks while you attend to people, handling the intense, complex, and unfamiliar, high-variety situations.

> Part of Stuart's job as division head was to deal with suppliers. He was the one who was supposed to make purchase decisions, but he wouldn't meet with the sales reps. He would tell his secretary to tell reps he was not in and then he would force one of us to hear the sales pitch. The only problem was that

none of us were in a position to make purchases. So needless to say, we never had the software or the hardware we needed in the company. Stuart should have met with the reps; he would have known if they were peddling the good stuff or not. By the time he got the information secondhand from us, it was all jumbled. *(accountant, male, age 35)*

Prepare for the Pop Quiz

Private affirmation of the anxious boss is not enough to get him or her to trust you. Anxious bosses will need positive proof of the sincerity and genuineness of an employee's friendliness. So they will test you—in public. They will watch for differences in your private versus your public attitude toward them. The boss will be exquisitely aware of any indifference, patronizing behavior, or contempt on your part. Therefore, the employee must be ever-sensitive and mindful, building the boss's feelings of confidence in himself or herself as well as in the employee.

Value Their Vacillation

Because of the anxious boss's need to avoid alienation in the office, he or she will either consider all or none of the suggestions offered by competing parties. One advantage of the first tactic is that the anxious boss is likely to gain a good understanding of the situation at hand before prematurely rushing off to make a half-informed decision. This is advantageous from the employee's perspective. But remember, when presenting your side, try to minimize conflict, appear rational, and convince the boss you know he or she will do the right thing.

Proceed with Caution

When working for an anxious boss, it is wise to remember the following maxims:

1. The more unfamiliar the situation is, the more anxious the boss will be.

2. If the situation appears to be totally novel, the boss is likely to panic.
3. If the boss starts to panic, he or she will distort reality and start imagining the most absurd "what-if" scenarios.

Therefore, anything that you can do to relate the situation to something that has happened before will be appreciated by the anxious boss. For example, say, "This is similar to that issue we encountered last year when . . . ." It doesn't matter whether this situation is very similar. You have to convince the boss the scenarios are the same. You have to bring the boss back to a familiar comfort zone. And you have to do all this without the anxious boss knowing what you are doing—that is, trying to work through the defect.

In the End:
Beyond the Dysfunction

Education makes a people easy to lead, but difficult to drive; easy to govern, but impossible to enslave.

Henry Peter Brougham

Understanding your boss and knowing how to maneuver around his or her defects will not change your leader, but it will change you. It will help you survive the psychological warfare raging in your workplace, and it will prevent you from losing your sanity. But that is as far as one might hope to go. To expect your boss to ever earn a clean bill of mental health is futile. To expect to turn the boss into a stalwart ally is a pipe dream.

Let's assume that you have diagnosed your defective boss, you have followed the prescriptions for persevering, and now you feel ready to take that next step—that is, you are ready to move on from just making the workplace tolerant to trying to make it somewhat pleasant. Our advice would be to move with caution. We have seen those who wanted to go beyond just understanding to helping their boss. This posture assumes, perhaps erroneously, a couple of things. First, that the boss cares how you feel, and second, that the boss won't later hold anything you say against you. These are dangerous assumptions.

Relationships with family and friends are characterized by mutual concern and respect. We encourage the growth and trust the integrity and motivations of the other. But perhaps more important, loved ones understand and tolerate our needs and desires. We are accepted and confirmed for who we are. This is not necessarily true at our place of employment. Although we would like to believe that the workplace is an enlightened and accepting environment, little evidence supports this. We would like to foster the spirituality of organizations, and although we know the office or shop could be a better place, trying to move it in that direction can be risky business.

Although this advice runs contrary to many of the best-sellers lining the shelves in bookstores, we believe that the pervasiveness of defective bosses is underestimated. We don't think the world of business has become that warm and fuzzy place we all so desperately long for. This is perhaps discouraging, but as Albert Einstein once noted, "Everything should be made as simple as possible, but not simpler." Organizations are still (to a large extent) complex, impersonal entities that value survival above all else. Sometimes individuals are sacrificed for the greater good, and your boss is in a position to ensure you can be slated for extinction—thrown alive into the burning corporate volcano, if you will.

When we are fortunate enough to be working for an effective boss, it might be possible to engage in some authentic self-disclosure about who we are, where we are going, and what we want to be. Indeed, an effective boss is likely to be concerned with our well-being. Effective bosses are essentially trustworthy, so we can have faith that they will not take advantage of our economic dependency. However, it is very tempting to a defective boss to use information we reveal about our dislikes and our shortfallings against us. This is particularly true if the boss knows that you know about or are trying to manipulate his or her defect.

IS THE BOSS BANANAS OR IS THIS A NUTTY PLACE TO WORK?

We constantly underestimate how much people's behavior is influenced by the situations they are facing.

Abraham Lincoln

Playing the role of "intuitive psychologist" is something we all are tempted to do. We observe someone acting in a way we never would and we ponder what sort of genetic mutations are occurring in their gray matter, what evil lurks in their soul. And when we come right down to it, we make attributions about their personality. For example, if we see a driver whizzing by us in a sporty red car, we label him or her as "aggressive," rather than assuming the person is late for an engagement. When we are attacked by a salesperson at the used car lot, we likely see him or her as a "vulture," rather than as an employee who is being manipulated by unrealistic sales quotas and unfair commission payments. When we are warmly greeted by a flight attendant, we believe the person is truly friendly. We never suspect he or she is simply doing no more or no less that the employee policy and procedures manual says the attendant has to do.

In short, when we observe the behavior of others, we make judgments about their personalities and ignore the situation that might have created their responses. This is often the case with our bosses. We watch their aberrant actions and their bizarre behaviors and immediately label them flawed. And they probably are. But how did they get that way? Why is the flaw becoming increasingly preeminent?

One could make a reasonable case that, even if bosses weren't born defective, the contemporary labor environment could make them so. Over the last decade, more than six million jobs have been eliminated, sometimes at the rate of over 3,000 per day. Many of these positions were from the ranks of management. "Redeployment," a benign term for layoff, has broadsided bosses. In fact, more than 15 percent of all middle managers have lost their jobs in the last few years. A betting person would know the odds are not in management's favor.

A funny thing has happened on the way to the unemployment line. We are finding, with greater and greater frequency, that those who got the ax earlier actually adjust better mentally than those who were "lucky" enough to stay on the job waiting for the next ax to fall. In fact, those who have outlived downsizings have suffered from such consistent physical and mental problems that we now have a name for their constellation of symptoms. We call it "Layoff Survivor Sickness," and it can stir up otherwise deeply concealed personality defects.

It is important to recognize that "Layoff Survivor Sickness," or the like, does not give birth to personality defects. We know personality is formed at a relatively early age, and that once formed, our character is relatively stable. But in placid environments, where there is stability and relative tranquility, defective bosses can adjust more easily. They can better repress their personality flaws and operate as a facsimile of normality. But in an economic revolution, where their basic security, status, and power are threatened, bosses resort to their basic instincts— to the root of their most primitive defenses. This is when we see the defect in all of its unglorious light.

At this point, you might be wondering why we have spent twelve chapters bashing defective bosses only to turn around and defend them in the end. The answer is simple. We are not defending them. We are merely suggesting that the work environment is now suited, and will continue to be suited, for the rise of the defective boss. Gone are the days of job security and implied lifetime contracts. Gone are the days when it seemed impossible for the organization to get any leaner. We will never return to the glory days, when the only unemployed people were those who didn't want to work or those who lacked the skills to find gainful employment. These are the days of insecurity and mistrust. These are the days of the defective boss.

So take cover. Don't passively wait for your defective boss to self-destruct. Rationality may not prevail. Even if it does, and your boss is "redeployed," there is no guarantee that you won't inherit another defective boss, or a more defective one. Trying to help your boss may be even less hopeful. You might find yourself in a situation of "codependence," which occurs when otherwise normal people invest so much time trying to heal other's defects that they become ill-focused themselves.

Your loyalty cannot rest with your boss or even your organization. Organizations do not want, nor will they accept, personal responsibility for you. This is becoming more and more evident. One-third of U.S. employees were dissatisfied with their workplace at the beginning of the 1990s. Today, one-half are alienated. The only option, and perhaps one of the most enlightened suggestions offered here or anywhere else, is to stop looking to others for career nurturance. Instead, take sole responsibility for your growth and development.

Many are realizing that the nature of the relationship they have with their employers is changing. It is no longer interpersonal; it is contractual. Employees have discovered that their dedication and loyalty were not reciprocated by their organizations. They were betrayed. So rather than aligning with their companies, employees are beginning to align with themselves. It is a different, perhaps difficult, way of doing things. But it is necessary for self-protection. The boss of old—supposedly there to protect, shelter, and foster you—has disappeared.

It is important that you not deceive yourself about how defective your boss is. If you distort the reality of your work world, you may become alienated from your true self. Instead, you must realistically see the defective boss without exaggerating or minimizing his or her flaws. Only through such an honest assessment can you best decide how to resolve your difficulties and approach your future. If you do so, in the end, you don't have to feel as Lincoln did during those turbulent times: "I claim not to have controlled events, but confess plainly that events have controlled me."

Bibliography

Bartlett, John and Kaplan, Justin (Eds.) (1992). *Bartlett's Familiar Quotations: A Collection of Passages, Phrases, and Proverbs Traced to Their Sources in Ancient and Modern Literature,* Sixteenth Edition. Boston: Little, Brown, & Co.

Diagnostic and Statistical Manual of Mental Disorders III-R (1987). Washington, DC: American Psychiatric Association.

Josephs, Lawrence (1992). *Character Structure and the Organization of the Self.* New York: Columbia University Press.

Million, Theodore and George S. Everly, Jr. (1981). *Personality and Its Disorders: A Biosocial Learning Approach.* New York: John Wiley & Sons.

Index

Predictable reactions *(continued)*
  depressive bosses, 139-140
  description of, *x-xi*
  explosive bosses, 93-95
  histrionic bosses, 55-56
  masochistic bosses, 119-121
  narcissistic bosses, 10-13
  obsessive-compulsive bosses,
    80-82
  paranoid bosses, 40-42
  passive-aggressive bosses,
    106-108
  sociopathic bosses, 26-28
Procrastination, passive-aggressives,
    104-105
Projection
  depressive bosses, 140
  paranoid defense mechanism, 43

Reactive depression, 135-136
Reassurance, depressive bosses, 142
Recognition
  histrionic bosses, 53,57-58
  narcissistic bosses, 17
  paranoid bosses, 45
"Redeployment," 159,160
"Reengineering," 3
Rejection, anxious bosses, 146,147
"Renegades," 69
"Restructuring," 2-3
Ridicule, anxious bosses, 146
"Rightsizing," 3,108
Ritual behavior, obsessive-
    compulsive bosses, 87
Rules, obsessive-compulsive bosses,
    84

Sadism, masochistic bosses, 123
Sales, sociopathic bosses, 33
Scapegoat, masochistic bosses, 115
Seclusion, anxious bosses, 151-152,
    154
Self-centered bosses, types of, *x,*4-61

Self-destruction, authoritarian
    bosses, 74
Self-respect, explosive bosses, 96
Sexual harassment, sociopathic
    bosses, 32-33
Shame, depressive bosses, 140
Silence, sociopathic bosses, 31
Sociopath, term, 19
Sociopaths, self-centered bosses,
    *x,*4,19-34
Specialness, histrionic bosses, 60
Spousal abuse, explosives, 96
"Stuffed shirt," 79
Substance abuse, sociopathic bosses,
    32
Suggestions, narcissistic bosses,
    15-16
Superboss, 120
Supervision, problems arising from
    defective, 2
Supporting role, narcissistic bosses,
    16

"Teasers," 56
Temper tantrums
  explosive bosses, 90-91,95
  handling aftermath of, 98
  histrionic bosses, 52
"Theory X" perspective, 69
"Tight ship," 85
Tolerance, sociopathic bosses, 32
"Top dog," 29
Traits
  anxious-avoidant, 149-151
  authoritarian personality, 65,71-72
  dependents, 127-128
  depressives, 140-141
  histrionics, 50-54,55-56,59
  masochists, 116-117
  narcissistic, 7-9,11-12
  obsessive-compulsives, 75-79,
    80-83
  paranoids, 36-37,41,42,45
  passive-aggressives, 99,101,102,
    103-105,106-107,109

Order Your Own Copy of
This Important Book for Your Personal Library!

DEFECTIVE BOSSES
Working for the "Dysfunctional Dozen"

_____ in hardbound at $29.95 (ISBN: 0-7890-0580-8)

_____ in softbound at $14.95 (ISBN: 0-7890-0581-6)

COST OF BOOKS_____	☐ **BILL ME LATER:** ($5 service charge will be added) (Bill-me option is good on US/Canada/Mexico orders only; not good to jobbers, wholesalers, or subscription agencies.)
OUTSIDE USA/CANADA/ MEXICO: ADD 20%_____	
POSTAGE & HANDLING_____ *(US: $3.00 for first book & $1.25 for each additional book) Outside US: $4.75 for first book & $1.75 for each additional book)*	☐ Check here if billing address is different from shipping address and attach purchase order and billing address information. Signature_____
SUBTOTAL_____	☐ **PAYMENT ENCLOSED: $**_____
IN CANADA: ADD 7% GST_____	☐ **PLEASE CHARGE TO MY CREDIT CARD.**
STATE TAX_____ *(NY, OH & MN residents, please add appropriate local sales tax)*	☐ Visa ☐ MasterCard ☐ AmEx ☐ Discover ☐ Diners Club Account #_____
FINAL TOTAL_____ *(If paying in Canadian funds, convert using the current exchange rate. UNESCO coupons welcome.)*	Exp. Date_____ Signature_____

Prices in US dollars and subject to change without notice.

NAME _____

INSTITUTION _____

ADDRESS _____

CITY _____

STATE/ZIP _____

COUNTRY _____ COUNTY (NY residents only) _____

TEL _____ FAX _____

E-MAIL_____

May we use your e-mail address for confirmations and other types of information? ☐ Yes ☐ No

Order From Your Local Bookstore or Directly From
The Haworth Press, Inc.
10 Alice Street, Binghamton, New York 13904-1580 • USA
TELEPHONE: 1-800-HAWORTH (1-800-429-6784) / Outside US/Canada: (607) 722-5857
FAX: 1-800-895-0582 / Outside US/Canada: (607) 772-6362
E-mail: getinfo@haworthpressinc.com

PLEASE PHOTOCOPY THIS FORM FOR YOUR PERSONAL USE.

BOF96

For Product Safety Concerns and Information please contact our EU
representative GPSR@taylorandfrancis.com
Taylor & Francis Verlag GmbH, Kaufingerstraße 24, 80331 München, Germany

www.ingramcontent.com/pod-product-compliance
Ingram Content Group UK Ltd.
Pitfield, Milton Keynes, MK11 3LW, UK
UKHW040926180425
457613UK00004B/41